BLOCKCHAIN

An Illustrated Guidebook to
Understanding Blockchain

MINGXING XU, YING TIAN, AND JIYUE LI

Illustration created by He Kui, Xiang Yu,
Wang Kun, Li Yanyang, Gong Xue, Ma Shanshan

Translated by Jie Liu

Skyhorse Publishing

Skyhorse Publishing books may be purchased in bulk at special discounts for sales promotion, corporate gifts, fund-raising, or educational purposes. Special editions can also be created to specifications. For details, contact the Special Sales Department, Skyhorse Publishing, 307 West 36th Street, 11th Floor, New York, NY 10018 or info@skyhorsepublishing.com.

Skyhorse Publishing® is an imprint of Skyhorse Publishing, Inc.®, a Delaware corporation.

Visit our website at www.skyhorsepublishing.com.

10 9 8 7 6 5 4 3 2 1

Library of Congress Cataloging-in-Publication Data is available on file.

Cover design by He Kui, Xiang Yu, Wang Kun, Li Yanyang, Gong Xue, Ma Shanshan

Print ISBN: 978-1-5107-4484-4
Ebook ISBN: 978-1-5107-4485-1

Printed in the United States of America

CONTENTS

PREFACE

"Paving Our Way to Blockchain" by Wang Wei

The tech world of today changes so quickly, oftentimes at breakneck speed. Internet finance had its run for several years, and then Financial Technology (FinTech) took its place. After the rise of FinTech plateaued, Bitcoin emerged. Then when Bitcoin miners and speculators came together, Blockchain technology thrived, and so began a new community. Waves of new concepts—ones that had been previously unheard of—captivated us. And with this soaring innovation and progressive technology, a surge of unfound anticipation of what the future may hold consumed us—even if we didn't fully understand the technology.

As this community grew, tech geeks created esoteric terms and lingo to build industry barriers against outsiders. Yet, in doing so, these terms—filled with technical jargon and gobbledygook—only added to the confusion of those on the outside, further isolating them from the world. Over time, an unintended consequence occurred: they lost the ability to communicate with the layman. Still, the general public is eager to learn more about this growing community and technology, as they don't want to fall too far behind in what they likely see as the inevitable future of tech and finance.

With this kind of growing excitement and curiosity, I paid close attention to Bitcoin mining, the algorithmic logic of tech geeks and Blockchain prophets. In the face of all the changes in finance, art, science, technology, and society, we will closely follow these innovations. And even though this may ultimately lead to nowhere, the journey itself—one filled with great unknowns—is worth it alone. This is Blockchain.

In the summer of 2016, I took part in a three-day conference of Blockchain held on Necker Island in the Caribbean. Richard Branson, the famous hippie and entrepreneur, invited a dozen figures in various fields from different countries to discuss the application of Blockchain in the arms of waves and sunny beaches. Yes, it was indeed time travel. More than thirty people who had never met one another, with the background of governments, courts, intelligent systems, art, aerospace, and environmental agencies, came together. We held dozens of discussions on various subjects, including the capture of fugitives, prevention of money laundering, protection of artistic property rights, validation of transaction authenticity, corruption prevention, social elections, earthquake relief, and endangered species protection. While vividly feeling the concrete achievements in these fields, we were also experiencing a commonly applied logic: all discussions were results of spontaneous organization and cross cooperation based on big data analysis, without any authoritative organization or enterprise organizing the system and process. According to the words of a young man on the site, we were creating a brand new trust agreement, with all the participants writing programs restricting our own behaviors. There was no condescending god, king, government, or big company making central control, the world was still running, and more important, the revolution was happening. This young man was Alex Tapscott. He and his father, Don Tapscott, the writer of many bet sellers such as *Wikinomics,* had just published their new book *Blockchain Revolution,* now popular in China. In January of 2017, when Don Tapscott and I were guests together at an activity, I invited him to give a speech at the Chinese Museum of Finance this summer.

Almost none of those who attended the conference on Necker Island were technical experts or Bitcoin miners, and they knew nothing about hash algorithm and the issue of double spending. But we all discussed Blockchain confidently. The reason is simple: TV program producers do not need to know how TV signals are launched and displayed, and it is not necessary for mobile phone designers to understand technical principles of 4G (the 4-generation mobile communication technology) and functions of each component. Also, for consumers to make phone calls or watch TV, in-depth technical knowledge reserve is not essential. During the evening party on the last night of the conference, the host proposed an interesting game in which everyone gave a unique definition of Blockchain. Some friends from Africa and Germany even rapped to express their ideas. Several keywords used were "trust," "certificate," and "transfer of value." The Blockchain can realize the transfer of value and is the second-generation Internet beyond information transfer. Certainly, those were the perceptions at that time. Today, we have significantly enriched our understanding of Blockchain. Everyone has the right to comprehend Blockchain. Specific standard definitions are not required.

By March 2017, more than forty Chinese books on Blockchain could be found online. It is estimated that another hundred will be published by the end of 2017. Similar to the period when the Internet just entered China, the overflow of books on Blockchain is a significant initial signal of this tide. Various translation versions of "Internet" appeared at that time, such as "因特网" or "万维网," but they were finally replaced by "互联网." Geeks have widely used the translation of Blockchain as "区块链," but someday this translation might also be replaced by a better one. The Museum of Fintech initiated two rounds of discussions on its translation in 2016. Some counterparts and I preferred the version of "公信链." But I also agree with many friends engaging in financial supervision, who think under China's current situation, "公信," or "credibility" in English, may be misused by illegal fund-raisers, so it will be better to let regulatory agencies evaluate the credibility.

Blockchain originated from Bitcoin and was explored and generalized as its underlying technology. Bitcoin caused widespread concerns in society, particularly under China's utilitarian atmosphere, which sticks to making profits. It became widely used in finance and investment sectors and was also immediately under close supervision. Meanwhile, Blockchain technology emerged and formed a more extensive application space independently. Like Internet's TCP (Transmission Control Protocol) or IP (Internet Protocol), if you are not obsessed with decoding and coding, you will be aware that applying Blockchain technology enjoys broader and deeper applications than browsing the Internet or conducting e-commerce transactions. Many people consider Blockchain to be an enormous distributed ledger system. Everyone gets involved in keeping and checking accounts, and no one can tamper with the data. It makes sense, but the function of Blockchain is far more than certificate function for keeping accounts.

Blockchain is actually a kind of concept that replaces authority control and affect-based trust with technical design to establish a network structure in which all participants can become nodes and be involved in authentication, right confirmation, transaction, review, and adjustment. Features like transparency, low cost, fast speed, and broad distribution make it impossible for authorities to modify, forge, and ban records. We can imagine that in today's fields of business, art, law, technology, politics, and even society, such a network infrastructure of civilized society building on computing ability and technical structure is very different from its counterparts. Operating without human feelings, it gets rid of crazy dreams, bossy authorities, distorted monopolistic consortia, and blind conspiracies concerning populism. Therefore, commercial fraud and emotional deception will not apply.

Whether we like it or not, a new society driven by Blockchain is forming, which not only happens in such fields as Bitcoin and financial technology. This embodies the vast change in society and the revolutionary influence referred to by many. Although the anonymous person known as Satoshi Nakamoto is the cornerstone of this era, the accumulation of social big data, unprecedented breakthroughs in computing, a pluralist and complex social network, and especially the life attitude and spirit of free choice possessed by people born after the 1980s all contribute to the core foundation of the Blockchain society. It might be difficult for us to foresee the future pivot of the Blockchain society, but it does disrupt our existing lifestyle. Nowadays, the most important thing is not how we define Blockchain, but how to understand and enter the Blockchain society.

Geeks of Blockchain broaden our horizons and improve our logical thinking. The wide application of Blockchain can lead many learners and innovators to the Blockchain society.

On January 17, 2017, the world's first Global Blockchain Business Council, which involved both governments and commercial organizations, was formally established by 25 countries. Jamie Elizabeth Smith, the former spokesperson and special assistant of U.S. President Obama, issued the *Davos Declaration*. The first national team members include many influential figures, such as Senior Executive of the World Bank Mariana Dahan, former Estonian President Toomas Hendrik Ilves, former Prime Minister of Haiti Laurent Lamont, and former Economy Minister of Ukraine Aivaras Abromavičius. As one of the founding members of GBBC, the China Blockchain Representative Team serves as the leader of the Training and Accreditation Committee of Blockchain, which is a critical chance for China to be involved in setting standards in this emerging field. According to the agreement, GBBC is going to compile textbooks concerning Blockchain in 2017 and open free training courses to popularize Blockchain applications, which are supported by all walks of life. After this news released on the WeChat, 170 people across the country signed up for this course in just three days. Lecturers included the former Deputy Chairman of the China Insurance Regulatory Commission Wei Yingning, the first President of the China Blockchain Applied Research Center Xu

Mingxing, and the newly appointed President Deng Di. The first trainees will be certified with GBBC and the Museum of Internet Finance. At present, Shanghai, Zhuhai, and other areas have started the new training program. The popularization of the Blockchain concept and successful application of Blockchain require the active engagement of the new generation of entrepreneurs and the tolerance and care of supervisors. Invited by the compilers of this book to write this preface, I'd like to finish by noting that I cherish the valuable opportunity to impart cutting-edge technology to trainees. I hope we can work together to lay a solid foundation for the Blockchain society.

—Wang Wei
Chairman of the China Finance Museum

INTRODUCTION

"A Guidebook to Blockchain" by Guo Yuhang

The way we understand and shape the world has been changing, and technology is the primary agent of this change.

Over the past few years, Blockchain has drawn considerable attention with its mystery of invention, the staggering price of Bitcoin, and the top-level design of financial reforms. Now, many people sing highly of its potential, comparing it to that of the Internet.

One difficulty facing all technologies in the process of popularization is how to educate the public about the new technology. The same is true for Blockchain. At an early stage, the people in China's Blockchain community quibbled over the Chinese translation of "Blockchain." Why? Because translation of the term is the very first step in getting this technology across to people's minds. As the Internet is translated as "Hulianwang," literally meaning a web that connects one another, it is necessary to give Blockchain an abstract name in Chinese to allow laypersons to understand what it means. "Qukuai" means "block" in Chinese, and "lian" means "chain"; even though it can be a little bit confusing for those who have no idea of this new technology, this Chinese term for Blockchain has been chosen and accepted by the public, for until now, no better translation can be proposed. After the translation of the term was decided, books concerning Blockchain begin to spring up like mushrooms. Different from those professional books full of abstruse illustrations and incomprehensible explanation, this book will focus on giving ordinary readers a glimpse of what Blockchain is, how it works, and what it can do.

The good intentions of the authors are also embodied in this book, as evidenced by vivid pictures and plain language that make this technology easily understandable. When reading this book, readers will not only be able to learn a fashionable concept, but they can also obtain enough knowledge to impress their friends when discussing WeChat Moments.

Of course, the journey to popularize Blockchain technology is far from smooth. It still requires readers to learn more about its fundamental technical concepts. So I would like to suggest that you visit the Chinese Museum of Finance to see the Bitcoin mining machines and see why it is difficult to crack Hash code and learn the latest development trends in the Blockchain industry in order to keep abreast of the times. You may think that there is no need for you to master this complicated technology during your lifetime. However, even at first glance, this book will help you to embrace a new world and understand it can be a new way of recording history, registering rights, and understanding value transfer.

As one of the forerunners of the Bitcoin industry, Star Xu, with his technological accumulation of facts and acute insight, founded OKCoin, the most popular Bitcoin Exchange in China. To promote a wider application of Blockchain technology, he wrote and presented for us this book. I believe his effort will add more momentum to the dissemination of the technology of Blockchain.

—Guo Yuhang
Founder and co-CEO of dianrong.com

1.

THE ORIGINS OF BLOCKCHAIN

Definition and the Inevitability behind the Contingency

FinTech is a phenomenal concept. As the Internet and technical industries register rapid growth, innovative programs of the FinTech industry also are witnessing singular development, among which Blockchain technology is undoubtedly the most eye-catching. Blockchain is one of the most promising industries over the next five years, as well as an emerging field in which many financial institutions and leading banks around the world are competing and pouring investments.

Speaking of Blockchain, the problems we'd like to discuss first invlove some *whys*: Why is it so popular? Why do people believe that it can change the world? Before starting this chapter, I have read many books concerning this technology, like *Blockchain Revolution*, *Blockchain Finance*, *Commercial Blockchain*, *Blockchain Society*, and *Blockchain Reshapes Economy and the World*, in which many specialists illustrate reasons why Blockchain can boom. They present different perspectives, including economics, commercial development, human history, and technological change. I even get caught up in the glamour of Blockchain after perusing these excellent works. Therefore, I'm going to explain the origins of Blockchain and its uses from the following four perspectives: the evolution of the ledger, value transfer, credit cost, and technical innovation.

Fig. 1-1: Bookkeeping in the Paleolithic Age.

THE EVOLUTION OF THE LEDGER:
THE RISE AND FALL OF THE ACCOUNT BOOK

"Distributed ledger" is the most representative word to define Blockchain, the most cutting-edge phenomenal concept in the

Fig. 1-2: Bookkeeping in the embryonic stage: portraying and sketching.

21ˢᵗ century. First, from the perspective of the evolution of the ledger, let's explore the following two questions: Why was Blockchain invented? and How does distributed ledger technology have the power to transform our economy and society?

Back in the Paleolithic period, people kept accounts (like the number of animals they hunted or ate every day) in their heads tens of thousands of years ago. However, as the number of people in tribes grew, their productivity became higher, leading to producer surplus. At the same time, the economic demand of people was so complex that keeping accounts in mind no longer sufficed, and improved bookkeeping was needed.

Therefore, people invented two methods: simple characterization and pictorial drawing, which meant recording with various symbols and awing things that had happened, respectively. This was the beginning of bookkeeping.

Fig. 1-3: The origins of bookkeeping: keeping records by tying knots.

However, symbols and drawings, with their taxing and space-occupied features, also failed to keep pace with the growing demand for bookkeeping. Under such circumstances, maintaining records by tying knots was invented. This well-known method was documented in historical texts and secondary school history textbooks and defined forms of recording objects, quantity measure, and final results. In addition, several principles of book entry could also be found as used by this method. Thus, it was almost known as the origin of the account book.

In late primitive society, productivity reached a new high, surplus products increased, and the division among agriculture, animal husbandry, and handicrafts expanded, which contributed to the invention of words. Characters and other narrative forms were adopted as ways to record tallies, in which income and expenses were recorded in chronological order.

Fig. 1-4: The end of primitive society: current accounts.

By the early 5th century BC, the economic boom in slavery societies of ancient Greece and Rome made it possible for journal accounts and cash books in running accounts. With the classification of time, the names of products and people, and currency capital, these account books were very similar to the ledger of an account. This phase was known as the "single-entry bookkeeping period."

Fig. 1-5: Single-entry bookkeeping.

Now, let's move to the generally recognized double-entry bookkeeping. Double-entry bookkeeping, which has been widely adopted in China, originated from the Longmen account at the end of the Ming Dynasty and early Qing Dynasty and later developed into four-element bookkeeping. The earliest double-entry bookkeeping in the West can be traced back to the 12th and 13th century and was widely used by bankers and merchants. The double-entry system could not only calculate operating costs, but also produce capital and profits, ensuring the continuous operation of companies.

Fig. 1-6: Double-entry bookkeeping period.

The 19th century witnessed the explosive development of information technology. At that time, as an individual no longer served as the owner and operator of a company and the work to be dealt with became more complex, all officials had the demand of checking account books. For example, if I were the largest shareholder of a company but unwilling to operate it, then I could employ a professional manager to do this job.

At the end of a year when the financial report showed that my bonus share was 10 million yuan, I would say that I wanted to check the account book. However, the account book recorded that the money spent on advertisements stood at 30 million yuan, much more than my annual salary, which made me doubt the accuracy of this ledger.

To be prudent, I employed an accountant certified by a third party and asked him to be responsible for bookkeeping. It was the surging demand for accounting and distrust between the owner and the operation of a company that led to the appearance of accountants. Since then, the rapid spread of computer technology brought accounting to a new stage—Computerized Accounting.

Fig. 1-7: The 19th century: The appearance of accountants.

In a world of informatization, digitalization, and intelligence, although methods of bookkeeping are continually improved and innovated, we are still faced with such issues as information asymmetry and trust crisis. Put simply, how can you trust the account kept by an accountant or audit to provide correct information? Do you ever wonder if your company may collude with accounting firms to cook the books? Now, Block-chain offers us a new way to solve such issues—the underlying application of Bitcoins, which can be seen as a shared distrib-uted ledger.

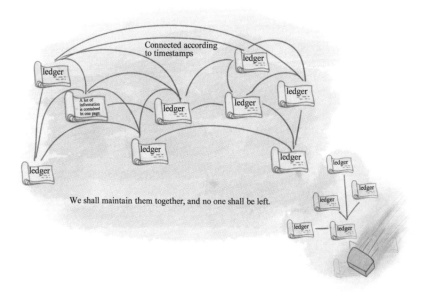

Fig. 1-8: The distributed ledger.

As a distributed ledger, Blockchain has the following features:

First, Blockchain is a huge ledger, in which every block can be regarded as a page, with a new page, including one or sev-eral entries, to be added for every new block.

Second, it is an encrypted and sequential ledger. All record information will be packaged into encrypted and time-stamped blocks, which are formed into a chronological, gen-eral account.

Third, it is a decentralized ledger that is jointly maintained by users in the network.

History has witnessed great changes in recording accounts. Now, thanks to technology, Blockchain has become the latest and most trustworthy form of bookkeeping.

VALUE TRANSFER: WHAT TO EXPECT AFTER THE INTERNET

The Internet, a concept that everyone is familiar with, has penetrated into every aspect of our lives. It serves as the information superhighway that can transmit all information with high speed and low cost except currency, a particular kind of information. Blockchain, however, is able to address this issue as a value transmission network.

Do you remember the story of the Internet? In 1993, the United States announced the establishment of National Information Infrastructure, a new project that was designed to build an information superhighway and enabled all Americans to

Fig. 1-9: The dawn of the Internet.

share and use information resources. This is the rudiment of today's Internet world.

Nowadays, everyone can produce information and spread it easily and swiftly. The rapid transmission of all information brings us to an age of information explosion. In order to satisfy people's need for diverse information, information transmission technologies continuously innovate, as evidenced by Cloud Drive and Automatic Network Replenishment.

It also begins to dawn on people that although most information like videos, photos, and audios can be used through copying and pasting, for some messages, reproduction is impossible and meaningless.

Fig. 1-10: How to transfer value.

For instance, it is impossible for payment to be completed through copying money. Instead, this process involves transferring money from payment accounts to collection accounts. A video can be posted on different websites and shared, while valuable assets that can be transferred but not shared often need credit endorsement. The Internet serves as a good tool for sharing information, but it can do little to deal with value transfer.

Let's explain this concept in a more straightforward way. Value transfer means a transfer of value or a set of values from site A to site B, in which the value reduced in site A is equivalent to the value increased in site B. As value transfer involves two independent parties, A and B, this process will be recognized, and cannot be manipulated, by both. However, current value transfer is often endorsed by a centralized third party rather than transmitted directly because this process cannot be finished by current Internet protocol.

Fig. 1-11: The centralized third party.

Through the endorsement of governments or companies, the current centralized institutions often deal with the calculation of value transfer in a central server, a process that inevitably involves the "infinite theory" and "opportunistic behavior" of humans, thus putting the credibility of the whole system at risk. Here comes the most fundamental question: how to reach consensus on credit?

Then Blockchain technology emerges, as the times require. Blockchain spreads all over the world and makes it possible for secure payments on an open platform across a long distance, and once completed, transactions will go into Blockchain as a permanent database.

What's more, all authorized parties in the network can share the same ledger. Once the ledger is altered, the modification of all replica data will be completed in minutes or even

Fig. 1-12: Credit consensus on Blockchain.

seconds. Every transaction in distributed ledgers has a unique timestamp to avoid duplicate payment.

Blockchain has established a pure peer-to-peer value transfer system. Even without mutual trust among nodes, it can ensure the integrity and security of recorded data in the system and do away with the endorsement of the third party, effectively reducing the complexity and risk of transactions.

Finally, I have to mention another feature of Blockchain—programmability, an open technology. As the openness of the Internet has ushered in a new era, can we suppose that Blockchain technology will also help us explore a new world?

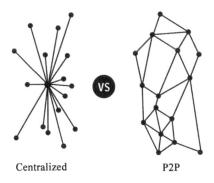

Centralized   P2P

Fig. 1-13: Centralization vs. peer-to-peer structure.

CREDIT COST: HOW MANY FACES CAN YOU REMEMBER?

Have you ever thought about this—how many faces can you remember? Have you ever heard of the incident of "Ezubao running away"? All these lead to the concept of "credit consensus." What will it cost to believe one man? Once institutions with public trust go wrong, what else can we trust?

In researching tribes, an anthropologist found the population of each tribe was always controlled around 150. The reason was that with more people, it would be almost impossible for them to remember the face of each kinsman, so they would not feel close to one another. Without intimacy, there would thus be no trust, and then endless battles and disputes among tribes could arise.

Fig. 1-14: The crisis of trust in the age of tribes.

In the age of tribes, it might just be one glance that would get you a good punch. But nowadays, in the era of the Internet, why do people tend to trust unknown, faraway merchants and even transfer their money to them? The reason is that during transactions, our trust has been resigned to national institutions and large-scale enterprises.

Although we still do not fully trust the sellers, we are willing to believe our nation and big companies with endorsements as the intermediaries. It serves as a common way to enhance mutual trust.

Fig. 1-15: The centralization of trust in the Internet era.

Among so many methods of increasing mutual trust, the most effective one to address the crisis of trust is Blockchain. As the core technology underpinning the Bitcoin financial system, Blockchain's essence is a growing distributed ledger database that can adequately resolve the trust issue in the information system. The issue comes from the following question: Why should you believe a stranger?

And why should others believe you? Blockchain uses an algorithm proof mechanism to secure the trust. With the help of Blockchain, every node in the system can exchange data automatically and securely in a trusted environment. Compared with other technologies that can be very costly and time-consuming, Blockchain has the advantage of real-time matching, automatic operation, compulsory execution, and low cost.

Technology is much more trustworthy than people. Blockchain technology brings us intelligent trust. Here is an example: Honduras has been troubled by domestic turbulence

Fig. 1-16: Intelligent trust brought by Blockchain.

and slack government administration. Thus, the registration information was often incomplete or even lost. The Honduran government solves this problem by applying Blockchain to configure a system for real estate contract registrations and transactions.

With the secure encryption technology of Blockchain, we no longer need to worry that our property rights are compromised due to the potential corruption of the government.

Fig. 1-17: Tampered property rights caused by government corruption.

In the future, all types of digital information can be added into Blockchains. As long as it can get into Blockchains, property rights can be clarified, protection conditions can be set, and transaction contracts can be formed automatically and executed forcibly. You do not need to worry about trust validation and execution, because Blockchain will do it for you. Next, we will take a look at the incident of Ezubao to discuss the issue of credibility.

In 2015, Ezubao, a P2P (peer-to-peer lending) company, was a rulebreaker. The company rose in a period of chaos and was destroyed by its crazy expansion practices using startling criminal means. This incident shocked the whole of China. Before being investigated, Ezubao advertised extensively during the prime time of every major satellite TV channel in China, which took advantage of the credibility of national television

Fig. 1-18: The incident of Ezubao. The Tragedy of Internet Finance behind the Ezubao incident [EB/OL]. [2017–05–18]. http://weixin. niurenqushi.com/article/2016–03–07/4176154.html.

to make endorsements for its high-risk Internet financial products. When a group of investors lacking professional knowledge met a crowd of heady ventures, the tragedy occurred.

In real society, transactions between people and companies need to be supported by credibility. Here, credibility refers to a kind of fairness, justice, transparency, humanity, and democratic trust shown in the social world when public power deals with time disparities, communication, and the exchange of interest. In our current society, credibility is usually provided by the government, state organs, and third-party organizations authorized by the government.

Blockchain enables credibility to be independent of third parties.

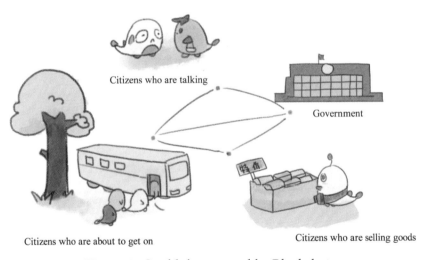

Citizens who are talking

Government

Citizens who are about to get on

Citizens who are selling goods

Fig. 1-19: Credibility created by Blockchain.

Blockchain technology can better satisfy the need for credibility and abstract credibility as independent entities instead of being controlled by the government or third-party organizations. Therefore, it can form a "new credibility pattern," achieving mutual supervision among government, the general public, Blockchains, and credibility. Trust is built upon Blockchains rather than being controlled by a single organization, so multiple parties can cross verify and cross supervise credibility.

What are the features of Blockchain credibility?

1. Since a Blockchain is distributed, credibility brought by distribution has various independent nodes on the network, each containing a copy of the backup information. Every authorized person can download all the data from any node. Meanwhile, credibility networks created by Blockchain is tamper-resistant. Attempting to change information from any node will be discovered by other nodes. And if a changed node is not confirmed, it will lose its credibility at once.

2. In the pattern of credibility brought by a Blockchain, Blockchain does not formulate any policy; it merely acts as a notary and government tool to establish and implement policies. Blockchain helps governments' policies to be accepted and recognized by the general public faster and more accurately. At the same time, since Blockchain refers to a fixed database that can duplicate, these policies become open and transparent.

From the perspective of trust, Blockchain uses consensual mathematical methods to build trust and complete credit creation among devices. Based on this feature, Blockchain also

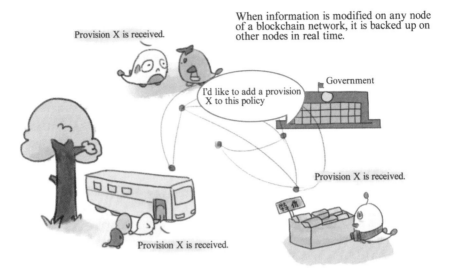

Fig. 1-20: A scene where Blockchain provides credibility.

shows the groundbreaking significance of promoting credibility. In *The Economist, John Smith* wrote, "the Blockchain is a device creating trust and its core is to address the issue of credit consensus, so to speak."

TECHNICAL INNOVATION: FROM BITCOIN TO BLOCKCHAIN

We all know that Blockchain is the underpinning technology of Bitcoin. It is also a pattern of distributed data storage or a public ledger that records transactions of cryptocurrency (like Bitcoin).

The transaction record is encrypted and held by all devices running this software. When we discuss Blockchains, it is natural to talk about digital currency, since Blockchains are created to meet the unique needs of Bitcoin. The concept of Bitcoin comes from a mysterious figure—Satoshi Nakamoto. In 2008, he published the article *Bitcoin: A Peer-to-Peer Electronic*

Cash System, which serves as the very basis of Blockchain technology and cryptocurrency.

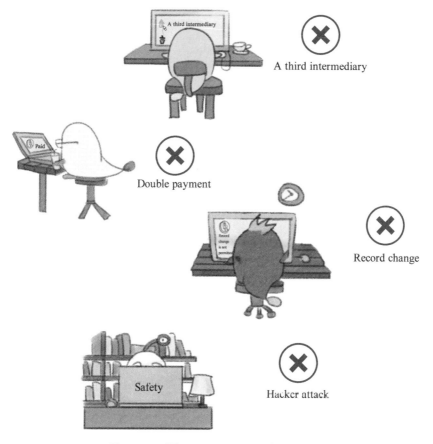

Fig. 1-21: The emergence of Bitcoin.

This article put forward several fundamental principles of Bitcoin:

1. A pure point-to-point electronic cash system enables one side to directly launch an online payment and pay the other side with no intermediary financial institutions involved.

2. The problem of double spending can be prevented without a credited third party. The point-to-point network environment is a solution that resolves double spending.

3. All transactions will be timestamped and merged into an extended proof-of-work chain based on Hash algorithm as transaction records. Unless all the proof-of-work is replicated in full, the established records cannot be changed.

4. The longest chain will be considered not only as the proof of the observed sequence of events, but also as the largest pool of maximum computing power from CPU. As long as most of the CPU computing capacity is not controlled by cooperative attacking nodes, the longest chain with its length exceeding the attacker can be generated.

5. The number of infrastructures required by this system is quite small. It only needs nodes to try their best to spread information within the whole network. Nodes can leave or rejoin the network at any time. The longest proof-of-work chain will become the proof of this node's transactions produced during the offline period.

When one considers all the viewpoints and logic above, the feasibility of the theory that point-to-point transactions can be realized merely through having the network act as a credit intermediary, with no centralized intervention or involvement needed, is convincing.

Based on such theory, the first Bitcoin transaction system, the first block ("Genesis block"), and the first case of paying by Bitcoin appeared. Bitcoin has operated smoothly for eight years so far without any serious technical errors.

Fig. 1-22: The smooth operation of Bitcoin for eight years.

In fact, as Bitcoin's underlying technology, the relationship between Blockchain and Bitcoin is more than "parent-child." Also, Blockchain is not an unexpected product of Bitcoin but was born synchronized with Bitcoin. And Blockchain reflects Bitcoin's availability and offers a broader possibility of interaction.

2.

THE THEORY

Consensus Creates Coded Trust

When I went back home on Spring Festival holiday last year, as a "festival routine," I was overwhelmed by all kinds of questions from my curious elder relatives. For example, What are you working on? When are you going to get married? How much can you earn every month? Usually, I can satisfy them with good answers, but this time, things were a little bit different. When I told them that I worked in a Blockchain technology company, 80 percent of them continued to ask, "what is Blockchain?"

I attempted to quote the definition of Blockchain on Baidu or Google and tried to explain to them the cool things we were doing with Blockchain. However, they responded with a more curious and confused facial expression. "Why can't you put it more simply?"

Then I realized that ordinary people can't comprehend the professional and rigorous definition on Baidu or in academic journals. I turned to Blog and Zhihu (the Chinese Quora) to try to find a simplified explanation. Among many articles on this topic, two interesting ones attracted my attention: one is the most-liked response under the hot topic "how to explain Blockchain to your stupid roommate"; the other is *Consensus on Blockchain*," written by Zhang Tongxie on Sina's blog channel. In the following part of this book, I quote some of their opinions and attempt to adopt their way of explaining—by telling stories—to elaborate on the definition of Blockchain.

WHAT IS BLOCKCHAIN?

Blockchain and Bikers

In 2006, financial giants like JP Morgan, Citigroup, Goldman Sachs, and NASDAQ all expressed their keen interest in Blockchain technology. What is this Blockchain technology (a.k.a distributed ledger)? We shall start with another story.

Before NASDAQ was founded, people use bikes laden with bonds around Wall Street for bond clearing and settlement.

Fig. 2-1: Bikers on Wall Street.

As businesses grew, bikes could not handle the increasing transactions. In the 1960s, Wall Street traded only four days, each day, for four hours, to help settlement keep up with trade volumes.

This practice could not continue. Bikes can never outperform computers. In 1971, people gathered together searching for solutions. DTC clearing system was then proposed. Under this solution, all transactions should be done with brokers included in this system, which is still adopted by NASDAQ. Obviously, this solution just replaced the bike with the "car." In many TV series, the country or the family is often trapped in chaos due to the death of the emperor or the head of the family. The cause of the plots mentioned above is that centralization is not enduring. When the number of transactions and brokers reaches a certain level, the system might be paralyzed or even crash.

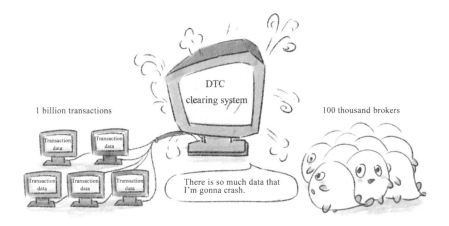

Fig. 2-2: Centralized DTC clearing system.

Blockchain is a distrusted ledger where every node displays and maintains the central ledger. The ledger cannot be tampered with unless someone controlled over half of the nodes. Take a simple example: You keep your family ledger and manage your parents' salary. If you want to buy some snacks, the ledger loophole is dozens of yuan. If you want to buy a cell phone, the loophole is thousands of yuan. This is just an example; I believe many of us in childhood desired pocket money from parents.

Fig. 2-3: Centralized family ledger.

With a distributed ledger, the above scenario will never come true. Everyone in the family participates in bookkeeping, and everyone can check the central ledger. No one can falsify the ledger. There is no money for your dad's cigarettes and your snacks.

Blockchain, in essence, is a decentralized and distributed ledger. It involves a set of cryptography-based data blocks.

Each block contains many pieces of information confirmed by Bitcoin's transaction network.

Fig. 2-4: Distributed family ledger.

Centralization and Decentralization

As we mentioned above, Blockchain is the decentralized distributed ledger. What does "decentralized" mean? First, let's picture in mind this situation: what will you do if you are buying a book online?

Step 1: Place an order and transfer a sum of money to Alipay.
Step 2: Alipay confirms receipt of the money and informs the vendor to deliver the book you ordered.
Step 3: The vendor receives the notification from Alipay and starts the delivery process.
Step 4: You receive the book and confirm receipt.
Step 5: Alipay receives your confirmation and transfers the money you paid for the book to the vendor.

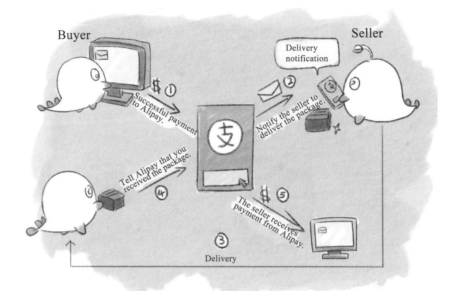

Fig. 2-5: Decentralized transaction process.

In the illustration above we can see that, even though the transaction happens between you and the vendor, Alipay is the true center of it. Therefore, the whole transaction process could

Fig. 2-6: Destruction of the central node leads to the failure of the whole transaction.

fail if something goes wrong with Alipay, such as a meteor crashing all the servers of Alipay, or a new round of global economic crises decimating Alibaba Group. Neither you nor the vendor could prove the transaction, which will lead to a dead end.

A Virtual City Running as Blockchain

To illustrate how Blockchain works clearly, we may as well propose an extreme situation based on the simplification of the decentralized and distributed construction. Assume that we have a decentralized city with five residents—we name them A, B, C, D, and E. Here is what they do when they want to borrow money from others:

Suppose resident B borrows one yuan from resident A, and A informs other residents by shouting, "I am A, and I just lent one yuan to B." Subsequently, B will say loudly, "I am B, I just

Fig. 2-7: Bookkeeping of a decentralized city.

borrowed one yuan from A." When other residents—C, D, and E—hear what they say, they write down on their ledgers, "dd/mm/yy, A lends one yuan to B."

Fig. 2-8: The impossibility of tampering with the distributed ledger.

In this extremely simplified model of a small city with only five residents, a distributed system is actually established in the city where no bank or Alipay is needed, which means that it works without a trusted relationship or credible organization. When every individual in this distributed system keeps their own ledger, it will be impossible to tamper with the records. Suppose B changes his mind and denies that he has borrowed one yuan from A? Then C, D, and E will testify on behalf of A using the same record on their ledgers—"dd/mm/yy, A lends one yuan to B."

Whether you noticed it or not, in this case, the money transferred from A to B doesn't really matter, because it can be replaced by any other concept of value that gets admitted by all people within the community. For example, resident A says, "I have created a Balala engergy," and when others hear that, they will record that A owns a Balala energy, even though they do not even know what the hell a Balala energy is. What next? Resident A can then say that "I transferred one piece of Balala energy to B." When all residents in the city, including B, C, D, and E validate the transaction, then this transaction will become officially valid.

Fig. 2-9: The circulation of Balala energy.

A Few Problems in Small Cities
Certainly, the Blockchain world will not be that simple. It also has other rules and restrictions. Let's first address the following issues:

Problem One: Why bother keeping a record?
Just because you shout to the sky, will others be obligated to help you keep a record? Does their time cost nothing? Do their

notebooks cost nothing? So, to fairly ask others to help me with bookkeeping, I added a new rule. I decided to reward the first person who heard me shout and recorded it in his notebook. The reward mechanism is also straightforward: the first one who heard me shout and recorded it can get a Balala energy reward. The Balala energy is not given to you; instead, it is the remuneration of your labor, just like earning money by working. You help me with bookkeeping, and the entire system will reward you. The requirements are as follows: First of all, you have to hear my shout and take it down before anyone else; after recording, you must immediately inform the whole city that you have finished recording this sentence and that neither you nor they have any use in rerecording it. This way, others will not try to profit by recording it themselves. In the meantime, you have to do one more thing, namely, adding a

Fig. 2-10: The reward for bookkeeping.

unique number to your record before calling it out along with the number, which enables the next person to continue with this record and the unique number.

When this new rule comes into operation, there must be people who, in order to get the Barrara energy, begin to hold their breath and listen to the shouts around them only to be able to be the first to take down a new record. Readers who know a little about the Blockchain might come up with the term "Bitcoin mining." That's right. This is a simple explanation of Bitcoin mining. On the topic of Bitcoin mining, a user of Zhihu named "Linglongxieseng" once mentioned a more vivid example in an article. The example is roughly this: when single men are looking for girlfriends, "national mother-in-law" would say something along the lines of, "I have a lot of beautiful and cute daughters who have pretty skin. If you can solve our troublesome problem, I will offer the WeChat number of one of them."

Fig. 2-11: The Universal "Troublesome Problem" of the "Mother-in-law."

Fig. 2-12: The reward for solving problems.

As a result, single men compete feverishly with one another, eager to solve the problem. As long as one of them solves a problem, he will immediately declare to the world proudly and demonstrate to everyone that the girl's WeChat number is his, persuading others to give up. Although the other single men have already set out, they are not fast enough and therefore have no choice but to solve the next problem at once.[1]

At the same time, the single lucky man who successfully solved the problem does not need to pay one or two hundred thousand yuan to pay for a bride; instead, the "national mother-in-law," conquered by his talents, would give him a vast fortune as a dowry, that is, the reward of Bitcoin in Bitcoin mining.

---

1   "How to explain Blockchain to your stupid roommate?" [EB/OL]. (2016–08–08) [2017–05–18]. http://mt.sohu.com/20160808/n463044051.shtml.

Problem Two: How to Deal With Forking?

We cite the description posted on Zhihu (the Chinese version of Quora) by the user, "Wangle-LaiW3n," in this section. In a large city, the problem will arise that B and C finish their recording and both of them yell to the sky at the same time, "The Balala Energy number 89757 belongs to me." However, the city is so large that some people claim that the Balala Energy number 89757 belongs to B, while others believe that it belongs to C. Nonetheless, the single Balala Energy number 89757 can be acquired by only one person. Therefore, how can we resolve the problem? Is it possible for each person to own half of the Balala Energy? Apparently, it is not acceptable. In this event, we will tackle this problem in an extremely primitive and simple way that lets the long information chain decide.

If there are no restrictions, the incident will develop as follows: some people believe that the Energy belongs to B, and they start adding to the record after hearing the claim.

Who is the No. 89757 Energy going to?

Fig. 2-13: How can we deal with forking?

Therefore, all their subsequent work will be done on the basis of the fact that B owns the Balala Energy number 89757. With the passing on of the information, the information chain will grow longer and longer. While for the other people who believe that C claims the ownership at first, the result is much the same.

The problem becomes exacerbated as the single entire information chain in a carefully numbered sequence diverts into two branches after B and C yell out their claim for the 89757 Balala Energy. If the problem cannot be solved immediately, each person will acquire his or her own version of the information, and no one will be able to figure out which is correct.

To solve the problem, the city adds new rules to the Blockchain. The record must be written in the top grid, and the distance of 0.89757 millimeters between the center of the record and the upper line of the matts should be guaranteed. Therefore, every person has to write after determining the right place with the help of ruler, which is highly difficult. The record takes each person five minutes to finish, and the time for taking down the sentence of claim differs from each other. Hence, others who are writing the sentence will

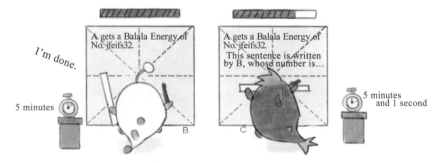

Fig. 2-14: Every time, the rules for recording are extremely intricate.

stop and begin another line that "the sentence is written by XYZ and the number of it is XXX" when someone else has yelled out, "I have finished. The sentence is written by XYZ."

Problem Three: Double Spending

Double spending refers to the phenomenon of the same digital cash being used twice in the same transaction.

If I yell to B and C at the same time, "I give you a Balala Energy," what can I do with the Balala Energy? There is only one Balala Energy, so how can I make sure that the single Balala Energy is used only once in the real transaction?

Take Bitcoin as an example. Satoshi Nakamoto clarified in the fifth section of the *Bitcoin White Paper* that the Bitcoin network runs as follows:

1. New transactions are broadcast to the network.
2. Each node brings the received transaction information into a block.
3. Other nodes will recognize the validity of the block when, and only when, all the transactions involved in the block are valid and appear for the first time.
4. Other nodes contend that they accept the block by following the end of the block and creating a new block to extend the information chain, considering the random hash of the block as the random hash of the new block.

In other words, timestamping has been added to the transaction data of Bitcoin since the beginning of the transaction, with the confirmation finished when the transaction data are packaged into a block. After confirming for six consecutive times, the transaction becomes irreversible. For Bitcoin, each confirmation is required to "solve an intricate problem." That is to say, every confirmation takes a certain amount of time.

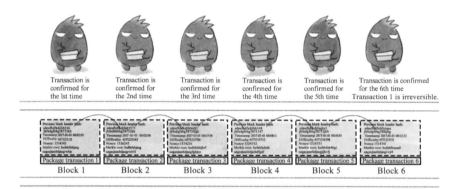

Sextuple confirmations are done, and transaction is irreversible.

Fig. 2-15: Irreversibility after six confirmations.

In this case, when I try to reuse the fund to pay for the transaction, it is nearly impossible for me to realize the confirmation of two deals at the same time because of the long time that is required by the confirmation. And the second deal cannot be confirmed after the first deal is confirmed as valid. The record of Blockchain throughout the network can be achieved without the problem of double spending on the condition that an agreement is reached across the entire network.

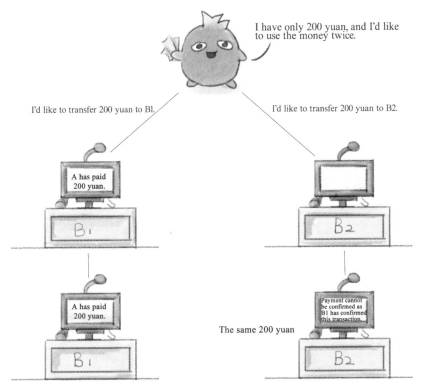

Double-spend problem is avoided.

Fig. 2-16: Double spending will not happen.

HOW DOES BLOCKCHAIN WORK?

The Core Concept of Blockchain

Before explaining the working principles of Blockchain, let us first make a brief introduction to several core concepts involved in Blockchain.

A. The Block

A block, as a basic structural element of Blockchain, consists of a block header containing metadata, and a block body containing transaction data.

The block header contains three sets of metadata:

1. Used to connect front blocks and index hash value data from the parent block;
2. Mining difficulty, Nonce (random number, a counter used for workload proof algorithm), timestamp;
3. Can summarize and quickly sum up Merkle root data of all transaction data in the check block.

Parent block hash

Mining difficulty, Nonce, timestamps

We are block headers, and no one shall be left.

Merkle root

Fig. 2-17: The structure of a block header.

Every ten minutes, one block can be created in the Blockchain system, which includes all the transactions' information that took place across the network during that time. Each block also contains the ID (identification code) of the previous block, which allows each block to find its previous node so that a complete chain of transactions is formed. Since its inception, the whole network has formed only one master blockchain.[2]

2   YANG Xiaochen, ZHANG Ming, "Bitcoin: theory, characteristic and vision" [J], Financial Review, 2014(2).

B. Hash Algorithm

Hash algorithm is a one-way password mechanism in the Blockchain to ensure transaction information is not compromised. After receiving a plaintext, Hash algorithm converts it into a shorter length and fixed-sizes hash data in an irreversible way.

It has two characteristics:

1. The encryption process is irreversible, which means that we cannot reverse the original plaintext by outputting the hash data.
2. Entering the plain text and outputting hash data correspond with each other, which means that any change in the input information will inevitably lead to changes in the final output of the hash data.

Fig. 2-18: Two characteristics of the hash algorithm figure.

In Blockchain, block encryption is usually performed using the SHA-256 (Secure Hash Algorithm), which has an input length of 256 bits and outputs a string of random hash data of 32-bytes.[3]

The Blockchain encrypts transaction information in a transaction block using Hash algorithms and compresses the message into a hash string of numbers and letters. The hash value of Blockchain can uniquely and accurately identify a block. Any node in Blockchain can obtain the hash value of this block through a simple hash calculation, and the calculated hash value does not change, which means that the information in the block has remained uncompromised.

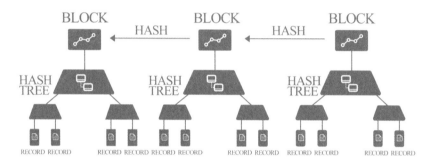

Fig. 2-19: Hash algorithm in Blockchain.

C. The Public Key and Private Key

On the subject of Blockchain, we often hear the expressions *public key* and *private key*. These are commonly known as asymmetric encryption, which is an improvement over the previous symmetric encryption (using the username and password). We use the e-mail encryption model to briefly introduce the public key, which is for everyone to use. You can publish by e-mail and let others download through the site. In fact, the public

3   TANG Wenjian, LV Wen, "How Blockchain redefine the world," [EB/OL]. (2017–02–24) [2017–05–18]. http://www.jianshu.com/p/89275ffca97b.

key is used to encrypt/verify the seal. The private key belongs to you only, and you must be very careful to keep it, preferably with a password. The private key is used to decrypt/sign and is owned by the individual.[4]

Public key and private key in Blockchain

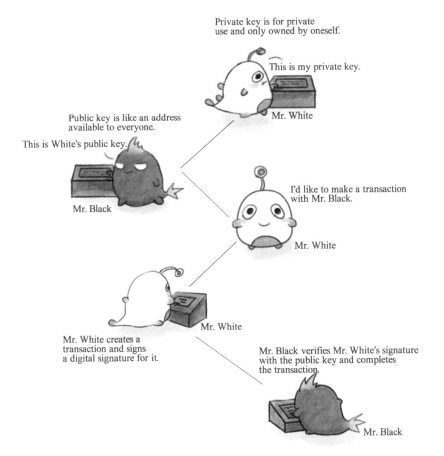

Fig. 2-20: Public and private keys in Blockchain.

4   Mosquito eats frog (nickname), "Public and Private Key" [EB/OL]. (2013–01–09) [2017–05–18]. http://www.cnblogs.com/wenzichiqingwa/archive/2013/01/09 /2853188.html.

In the Bitcoin system, the private key is essentially an array of 32 bytes. Both the public key and the address are generated based on the private key. With the private key, the public key and address can be generated, and the Bitcoin on the corresponding address can be spent. To spend via Bitcoin using a private key is to sign the unspent transactions to which it corresponds.

In Blockchain, the public key and the private key are used for identity identification. Let's assume that there are two people in Blockchain, Tom and Jerry. If Tom wants to prove that he is really himself, he only needs to use the private key to sign the file and send it to Jerry. And then Jerry uses the public key to verify the signature of the file. If the verification succeeds, it proves that this file must be encrypted by Tom with a private key. As Tom's private key can only be held by Tom, it can verify that Tom is really Tom. In the Blockchain system, the public key and the private key can also ensure the security of

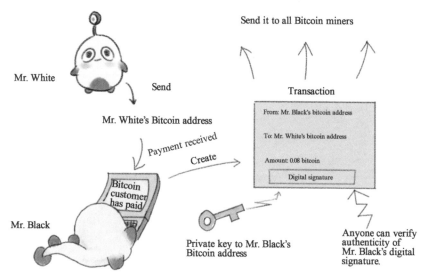

Fig. 2-21: Using the public key and private key to complete a transaction.

peer-to-peer information delivery in distributed networks. In the Blockchain information transfer, encryption and decryption of both public and private keys of information delivery are often unpaired.

For senders, the private key is used to sign the information, and the information receiver's public key is used to encrypt the information. For the information receiver, the sender's public key is used to verify the sender's identity, and the private key is used to decrypt the encrypted message.

D. The Timestamp

The timestamp in Blockchain exists in the block from the moment the block is generated. It corresponds to the authentication of each transaction, proving its authenticity. Timestamps are written directly in Blockchain, and the blocks that have been generated in Blockchain cannot be tampered with, because once tampered with, the generated hash value changes and becomes an invalid datum. Each timestamp will

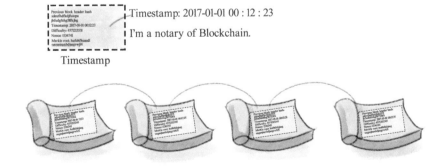

Fig. 2-22: Timestamp in Blockchain.

also include the previous timestamp in its random hash. This process is repeated, sequentially linked, and finally produces a complete chain.

E. Merkle Tree Structure

Blockchain uses the Merkle tree's data structure to store the values of all the leaf nodes and uses that as a basis for generating a uniform hash value. Merkle tree leaf nodes store hash value of data information, while non-leaf nodes store hash value of the combination of all leaf nodes below them.[5]

Similarly, the change of any one datum in the block will lead to the change of the Merkle tree structure. Merkle tree structure can significantly reduce the amount of data computation

Merkle tree

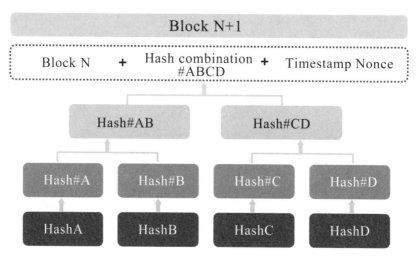

Fig. 2-23: Merkle tree structure in Blockchain.

---

5   Mosquito eats frog (nickname), "Public and Private Key" [EB/OL]. (2013–01–09) [2017–05–18]. http://www.cnblogs.com/wenzichiqingwa/archive/2013/01/09 /2853188.html.

in the transaction information verification comparison, for all we have to do is to validate the uniform hash value generated by the Merkle tree structure.

When speaking of the Bitcoin virus, we have talked about several core concepts and definitions of Blockchain, but how does it work? To solve this problem, we have to start talking about Bitcoin, at which point many people's first reaction is to bring up Bitcoin virus. To approach the topic of the Bitcoin virus incident, we must first talk about what exactly Bitcoin is and its characteristics, describing what the whole world knows. Remember the fear of being dominated by Bitcoins?

On that day, when you woke up in the morning, you found an ugly red frame pop up on the screen. You were so excited because, finally, you did not need to write essays.

Fig. 2-24: Bitcoin virus invasion.

On May 12, 2017, a trivial incident occurred online. Documents in many schools and hospitals were locked up by a ransomware worm called "EternalBlue" (also known as WannaCry). It stated that if you want to see information, you need to pay. Not too much, 300 Bitcoins. At first glance, someone may think that it is only 300, so few. Actually, the price of a Bitcoin is almost equal to 10,000 Chinese yuan in China, because the Bitcoin platform is under regulation in China and therefore cannot be withdrawn. The price in other countries is even higher. Of course, for individual users, it is not necessary to give so much money; after all, not everyone has over 300 million yuan.

Give me 300 Bitcoins, and you can open your files.

Fig. 2-25: Bitcoins are required to unlock.

Hackers want everyone to pay in Bitcoins, but that is not really the problem with Bitcoin. Bitcoin is a coin, lying quietly aside, waking up in the morning to find itself in the headlines. Till May 16, 2017, more than 300,000 users in over 150 countries have been "persecuted." Moreover, it is said that the "EternalBlue" virus has been upgraded to version 2.0, which is not limited by the domain name, with higher dissemination.

Fig. 2-26: "EternalBlue."

So, what is the Bitcoin virus? It can be regarded as a magical virus, a mixture of two things—the encryption algorithm blackmail virus and the "EternalBlue" hacking tool. The "EternalBlue" hacking tool is responsible for entering people's computers without a click, and then the encryption algorithm blackmail virus encrypts your files before blackmail. Where does the Bitcoin virus come from? The encryption algorithm blackmail virus is actually an "old friend." Cryptolocker, the world's first recorded ransomware, was born in 1989 as a program that uses cryptographic algorithms to blackmail money. The virus maker was apprehended in a few days.

Fig. 2-27: The maker of the Cryptolocker virus was caught.

In fact, Cryptolocker is very simple to solve at the beginning, because it uses a symmetric encryption algorithm, which is cracked easily by a reverse program. However, the ransomware virus, like Wallet and Onion, currently uses an asymmetric encryption algorithm. The encryption and decryption pro-cesses of asymmetric encryption algorithm use two different keys, so simply reversing the program is not feasible, which we will explain in detail later. However, this time the hacker not only improved the ransomware worm, but also equipped it with a "good companion"—the "EternalBlue" hacking tool—which can directly occupy your computer without your click-ing on any link. There is also the beautiful legend of the "Eter-nalBlue" virus, which is said to have been used by the National Security Agency to steal information from other countries and is in the "arsenal of the United States."

Fig. 2-28: The irreversible charateristics of asymmetric cryptographic algorithm.

The U.S. National Security Agency has a hacker organi-zation called "Equation Organization," which is responsible for classified works for the U.S. government that cannot be cracked by reverse programs.

Fig. 2-29: The Legend of the "U.S. Arsenal."

Later, the organization became known because of the world-famous "Stuxnet" incident in the Iran nuclear test and "PRISM" incidents. Subsequently, a hacker group called "Shadow Brokers" cracked the "arsenal of the United States."

Fig. 2-30: The Legend of the "Shadow Brokers."

They held auctions online, selling these "weapons" with money, but no one was interested. Then, they launched crowdfunding, wanting to make a profit from these "weapons," but still no one paid attention. Subsequently, on April 14, 2017, they released the "weapons" directly. Since then, the "EternalBlue" hacking tool and the encryption algorithm blackmail virus became "lethal weapons."

Indeed, this is just a beautiful legend, and the NSA did not admit it. Therefore, there are differing opinions about where "EternalBlue" comes from, and there is no practical proof. When can the virus be cracked? First of all, the "EternalBlue" hacking tool attacks Windows (Microsoft's operating system) loopholes, which means that as long as you update with Windows patches and turn on the active defense of the firewall, this tool does not have the soil to survive.

Fig. 2-31: Upgrading the firewall.

However, Windows always has new loopholes. Maybe the hacker equips the virus with a tool to attack a new loophole, giving birth to a variety of viruses, such as "EternalRed,"

"EternalYellow," or the like. As we know, ransomware virus uses asymmetric encryption algorithms for encryption. Its most prominent feature is that it cannot be tampered with or reversed. The encryption and decryption processes use two different keys.

Fig. 2-32: Hard to crack an asymmetric encryption algorithm.

Now, the computer cannot complete the amount of back-calculation required, because the cost is too high. Thus, the hottest Blockchain technology in the world is using asymmetric

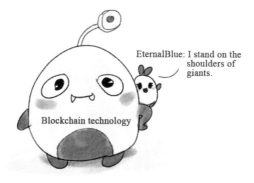

Fig. 2-33: Standing on the shoulders of giants.

encryption algorithms. That is to say, hackers design passwords on the basis of the most advanced technology of the times. It is not easy for us to crack them.

Recall how the well-known "Panda burning incense" virus was finally cracked. The hacker was caught and forced to write a program to crack it. This outcome remains the norm. The most likely solution is to catch the hacker and force him or her to hand over the key. After we enter the key, we can unblock it.

Fig. 2-34: The hacker hands over the key.

When and how will the Bitcoin hacker be caught? These questions involve a third question, which is why do hackers require payment in Bitcoins? The answer is that it is easy to get away with because of the anonymity of Bitcoin. Bitcoin is an online virtual currency that can circulate with anonymity, which makes it easier for hackers to hide their identity. You do not need to know who the other person is; a Bitcoin address alone allows you to realize point-to-point transfer. Another reason hackers choose Bitcoin is that Bitcoins are recognized around the world and can be circulated globally. Bitcoin accounts for the largest share of digital money. It has many "fans" around the world. Many countries recognize the legal status of Bitcoin, and some large companies even accept Bitcoin payments.

Fig. 2-35: Bitcoin's internationality.

However, it is not so easy for hackers to escape from the arm of the law because one of the characteristics of Bitcoin is that it can't be compromised. All records cannot be tampered

The hacker has published the Bitcoin address
"1A1zP1eP5QGefi2DMPTfTL5SLmv7DivfNa"
The payment has been received: start tracking now!

Fig. 2-36: Bitcoin transaction records are publicly available.

with and are publicly available. Once the address released by the hacker receives Bitcoins, a record is added to the ledger and everyone's ledger updates simultaneously. Everyone can find this record. The transfer of this address and cash withdrawal records are also verifiable. As long as the hacker conducts operations requiring interaction with realities such as withdrawal, it will undoubtedly reveal clues.

In fact, in most cases, Bitcoin business is not 100 percent anonymous. Transferring Bitcoins is similar to an author publishing his work under a pen name. If an author's pseudonym is associated with his identity, anything he has ever written is also associated. For individuals, the anonymity of Bitcoin is related to your wallet that receives Bitcoins. Every transaction involving this address is permanently stored in this Blockchain. If your address is related to your real identity, then every transaction will be related to you. Many countries are now monitoring the Bitcoin trading platform, and transactions require multiple real-name authentications.

Fig. 2-37: Bitcoin is not 100 percent anonymous.

Therefore, as long as any clue is found about the true information concerning, and consequently the identity of, the hacker, then he or she will be very likely to get caught.

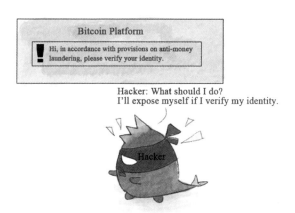

Fig. 2-38: Multiple real-name authentication.

HOW TO PREVENT THE "ETERNALBLUE" VIRUS

Solution One: Searching

Now, open any of your browsers, input "how to prevent Bitcoin virus" in the input box, and you will see overwhelming solutions pop out. You can click any one of them to read; they

Fig. 2-39: Solution one: searching.

all read the same. You simply cut off the Internet, set a firewall, block port 445, and update the Windows patches. I recommend that you get into the habit of opening up your firewall in the long run, though the Windows firewall pops out
from time to time. Security is paramount.

Solution Two: Fighting Fire with Fire

What should we do if it happens again? You can try this: What
the hacker tries to encrypt are our important files, the suffixes
of which are doc (documents), xls (spreadsheets), ppt (presen-
tations), psd (image files), etc. The hacker will not encrypt the
videos and seed files in some unpopular formats. Therefore,
in addition to backing up important files a few more times, we
can also make them into compression packages and change
them into an unpopular format like .modv. Of course, this cannot make the important files entirely immune to destruction.

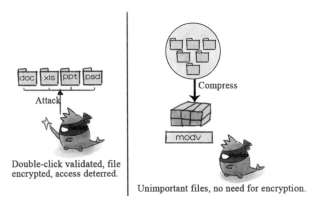

Fig. 2-40: Solution two: fire with fire.

Solution Three: Rob His Job

The best part of this move is that you can get the hackers
out of the way. This applies to programmers who can write
a "virus program" with asymmetric encryption to encrypt all

the files in personal computers. They can input the password each time before seeing the files, since the password is known only by themselves. It is a little messy, but it works: "It is mine; you can find no way to get to it."

Fig. 2-41: Solution three: rob his job.

The last thing to remind you of is that in China, Bitcoins cannot be withdrawn. Therefore, you should consider whether to pay ransoms prudently. After all, we cannot ensure there is no second invasion after the payment. Facing the virus, we should keep calm.

Fig. 2-42: Failure to unlock after paying the ransom.

Since I work in the Blockchain and Bitcoin industry, from the moment the virus broke out, I have received a lot of phone calls from relatives asking questions like "I heard that you study the virus, are you running away?" During the workdays, I am always being asked, "Please share your opinions, when can the manipulator be caught?"

The reason why hackers use Bitcoin for ransom is that it has features such as anonymity and decentralization that can help them to hide their identity. But I always hold the opinion that technology itself is innocent, and neither Bitcoin nor Blockchain should take the responsibility.

Bitcoin   Blockchain

We should let them take advantage of us, and technology should be to blame.

Fig. 2-43: Technology itself is innocent.

The Workflow of Bitcoin

As Fig. 2-44 shows, in Blockchain, all the nodes go back up to the source, which is also the first block of Blockchain—"Genesis block."

After the creation of "Genesis block," users of Bitcoin keep "solving the problem." By calculating, they try to get the numerical solution that meets the specific SHA-256 hash values.

This process is called "Bitcoin mining."

No matter which user gets the numerical solution meeting the requirements first, it will be broadcast through the

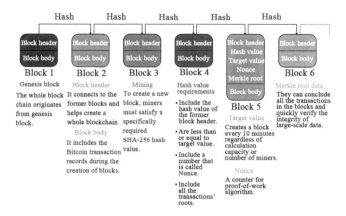

Fig. 2-44: The workflow of Bitcoin.

network. Then, other nodes will receive the information and validate it. Once it is validated, other nodes will stop calculating and add the new block after the previous one.

More and more users join the Blockchain system of Bitcoin, and more and more hash values are found. In the process of repetition, new blocks are continuously generated and validated. Finally, a main chain is formed. In the meantime, the difficulty of the hash algorithm is adjusted to control the time spent by users in getting the solutions.

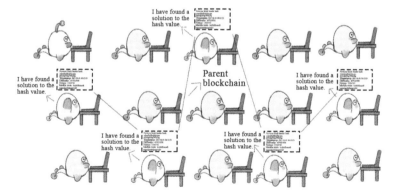

Fig. 2-45: Figuring out the numerical solution to meet hash values.

In the actual trading process of Bitcoin, assuming that user A and user B are going to make a transaction, the block with which broadcasts to all the users in the Blockchain allowing them to validate it. Once the transaction is validated, this block will have a timestamp and be added into the main chain of Blockchain.

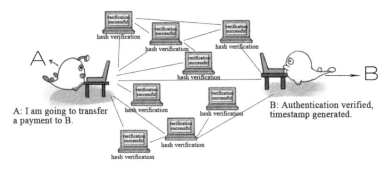

Fig. 2-46: Using a timestamp.

The essence of Blockchain is a public mutual validating accounting system, which records all transactions of all accounts. Each change of any account will be recorded in the general ledger. All the users have a complete ledger with which they can independently calculate all the accounts as well as the current balance of everyone.[6]

Since all the statistics are transparent, everyone can check the source code. In this way, people will trust the decentralized system without worrying about any hidden conspiracies.

---

6   BTSX Investment White Paper V1.1 [EB/OL]. (2014-09-16) [2017-05-18].http://www.docin.com/p-924681871.html.

BITCOIN HARD FORK

Since it was born in 2009, Bitcoin's market cap has climbed to tens of billions of US dollars, and many people are crazy about it (please note that according to China's policy, Bitcoin is not currency). Recently, some predict that Bitcoin may even plummet when a fork becomes ineluctable.

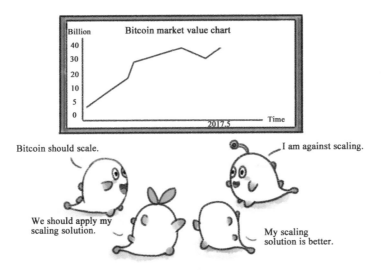

Fig. 2-47: Is a Bitcoin fork inevitable?

Satoshi's Decision

Back to 2009, when Satoshi was projecting Bitcoin, the data at hand were limited, so he decided the capacity of one block to be 1M (megabyte). However, one transaction occupies 250 bytes and even more. Some transactions even need 500 bytes. Apparently, the capacity is far from enough.

Let's do the math together:

One block's size is 1M, 1M=1,024KB=1,048,576B.

Then the number of transactions that one block can hold is

1,048,576÷250 ≈ 4,194.3.

The time to verify one block is 10 minutes, 10 minutes= 600 seconds.

Therefore, the number of transactions that can be verified per second is 4,194.3÷600 ≈ 7.

Fig. 2-48: 1M size is apparently not enough.

Every block is only able to verify seven or fewer transactions per second, which will undoubtedly lead to the congestion of transactions and thus low verification speed. Once one transaction has finished, it has to wait in a long queue to be

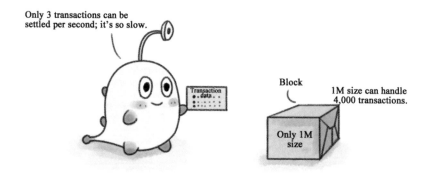

Fig. 2-49: The blocks need scaling.

verified. One day, the congestion will reach its limit and cause the whole system to break down.

Different Scaling Plans

How should we deal with the problem? Start to change!

How to change? Nowhere can we find Satoshi! Then to whom should we turn? Satoshi has entrusted the maintenance of Bitcoin system to five geeks!

Then again, how to change?

Listen to me: we should scale the block size to 2M.

No, it should be 20M.

Many people put forward their own scaling plan on behalf of their interest groups.

1. **Bitcoin Classic:** The maximum of this field should be scaled to 2M, and in the future, it is planned to take the median of the first 2,016 blocks and multiply it by a predetermined multiple to determine the upper limit of the size of the next blocks.
2. **Bitcoin XT:** The maximum should be 20M and doubled every two years until the upper limit reaches 8.3G (Gbyte).

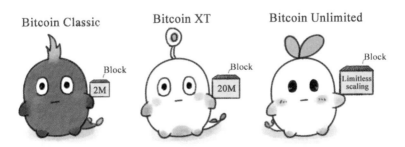

Fig. 2-50: Different scaling plans.

3. **Bitcoin Unlimited:** The maximum can be any number—even infinite—and the mining pool should determine its size.

No agreement has yet to be reached because each group believes their plan is the best. What should we do now? If we can create an upgraded version of Bitcoin and everyone agrees to join the new system, then there will be no need to fork. However, how should we get everyone to agree to upgrade?

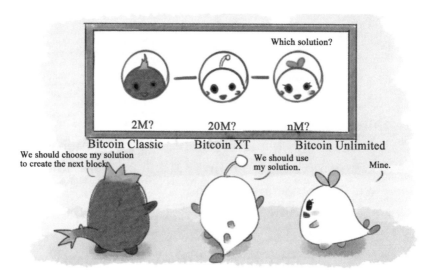

Fig. 2-51: Disagreement on scaling plans will lead to a fork.

Different opinions and ideas have given rise to a variety of scaling plans, and those plans cannot be unified. Thus, a Bitcoin fork becomes inevitable. In fact, in the future, the proposed size may grow even larger.

HARD FORK AND SOFT FORK

What is the difference between a hard fork and a soft fork? To put it simply, it is the difference in compatibility. A soft fork is temporary, and a hard fork is permanent. When permanent divergence occurs on Blockchain after new consensus is released, some nonupgraded nodes cannot verify the upgraded blocks—then a hard fork happens.

Hard fork

Fig. 2-52: Structure diagram of a hard fork.

Here is the definition of a hard fork: the situation where a parallel chain is added to the old chain after changes happen to Bitcoin's block format or transaction format, and the nonupgraded nodes refuse to verify the blocks that are created and verified by the upgraded nodes.[7]

Fig. 2-53: What is a hard fork?

7   "Bitcoin technical note: what is consensus, fork, and compatibility?" [EB/OL]. (2016–10–11) [2017–05–18]. http://business.sohu.com/20161011/n469963760.shtml.

Here are the characteristics of a hard fork:

1. No forward compatibility, and the previous version will be forced to upgrade.
2. There will be two parallel chains: the old one and the new one.
3. The nodes need to agree to fork at a certain point in time, and those that disagree will remain on the old chain.[8]

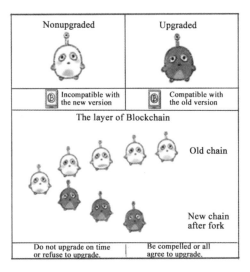

Fig. 2-54: The characteristics of a hard fork.

When a new consensus is launched, a temporary fork may occur because the nonupgraded nodes will create illegal blocks, since they do not fully understand the new consensus. Thus, the definition of a soft fork: when the data structure of Bitcoin transactions changes, the nonupgraded nodes can verify the

---

8   "Hard fork scaling has the risk of split while soft fork does not" [EB/OL]. (2016–10–09) [2017–05–18]. http://8btc.com/thread-40509-1-1.html.

blocks produced by the upgraded nodes, and the upgraded nodes can also verify the blocks produced by the nodes that have not been upgraded.[9]

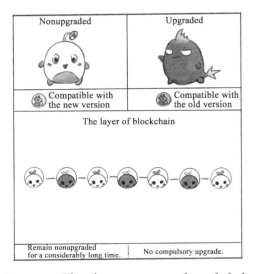

Fig. 2-57: The characteristics of a soft fork.

INTERESTING EXAMPLES

Let's take the restoration of a palace as an example. Suppose there is a Bitcoin kingdom on an isolated island, and the palace of this kingdom has withstood many years' erosion and started to appear dilapidated. Some ministers of the court suggest the king tear down the palace and rebuild, while some believe repair and restoration can make the palace look new. The two groups argue with each other, and neither can persuade the other, which leads to a fork.

---

9   "The growing pains of Bitcoin: solution to the problem of congestion or thoroughly split?" [EB/OL]. (2017-03-21) [2017-05-18]. http://forex.cngold. org/c/2017-03-21/c4886602_2.html.

Fig. 2-58: The example of a Bitcoin kingdom.

When will a hard fork occur? Because the two groups cannot reach an agreement, they decide to implement their plan separately. Those who propose to rebuild the palace hire workers

Fig. 2-59: Example to illustrate a hard fork.

to build anew, and those who insist on restoration keep the old part of the palace. This situation can be compared to the hard fork in Bitcoin's world when a new chain splits from the old chain at a certain point in time, and these two chains are not compatible with each other.

What will happen when a soft fork occurs? Let's get back to the Bitcoin kingdom. To prevent the argument between the two groups from reaching an impasse, they agree to compromise. Both sides can do what they wish to the palace and admit the legality of each other's practice. Similarly, in Bitcoin's world, when a soft fork occurs, the nonupgraded nodes can stick to the old rules, while the upgraded nodes will start to adopt the new ones. For example, after Segwit proposed by Bitcoin Core, no new coins were produced.

Fig. 2-60: Illustration of a soft fork.

WHAT IS THE INFLUENCE OF A FORK?

First, let's have a look at a recent, successful fork. In July 2016, the Ethereum development team forcibly transferred all funds of The DAO (Distributed Autonomous Organization) and its sub-DAOs to a specific refund contract in Block 192,000 by modifying the code of Ethereum Software. The address thus "recaptured" the ethernet currency of the DAO contract controlled by the hacker. After that, two chains were formed, one for the ETC (original chain), and the other for the new ETH (new chain). Then a hard fork happened!

Fig. 2-61: Ethereum's hard fork.

It had a massive influence on miners: mining can be easier for them after the fork, but the price of coins will be more unpredictable because of the uncertainty in the market afterward.

The mining speed on the new chain is faster.

But not many people are trading this currency, so its price is pretty low.

Miner   Miner

Fig. 2-62: The impact on miners.

A Hard Fork's Impact on the Bitcoin Industrial Chain

From a technical point of view, the main problem with a hard fork is that it requires all users to move to a new Blockchain with different rules. In order to maintain the brand value of Bitcoin and people's faith in Bitcoin, Bitcoin's supporters are opposed to hard forks. If a hard fork really happens, it may set off a cyberwar and a consensus war.

A Hard Fork's Impact on Bitcoin's Price

The market determines the price fluctuation and outlook of Bitcoin. Theoretically speaking, Bitcoin prices will first undergo a slump after a hard fork.

Join in the new chain! We have made new rules.

We think the old chain is good and will not join the new chain.

Users of the new chain

Users of the old chain

Fig. 2-63: The impact on an industrial chain.

Both Bitcoin and the new coin occurring after the fork will return to a normal level. The discussion of a Bitcoin fork shows no sign of ending. Maybe this is precisely the glamour of decentralized Bitcoin—the diversity.

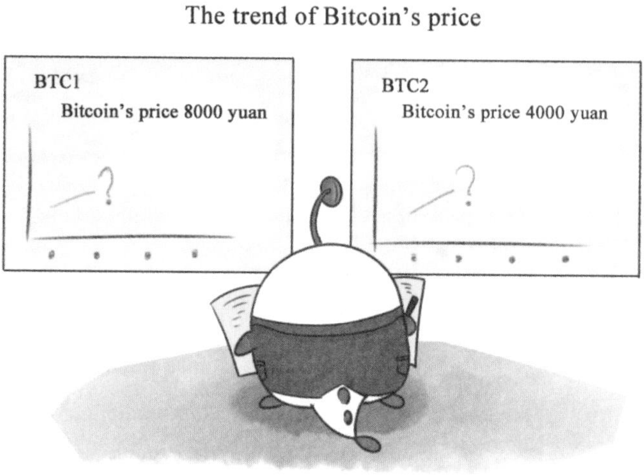

The trend of Bitcoin's price

Fig. 2-64: The impact on Bitcoin's price.

THE WORKING PROCESS OF BLOCKCHAIN

How does Blockchain work?

As Fig. 2-65 shows, assume that A and B are going to have a transaction. A launches a request of setting up a new block, and the block will be broadcast to all the users in the network. After validated by all the users, it will be added to the main chain, which saves permanent and transparent transaction records that can be checked by every user. Actually, the Blockchain technology is a distributed database in which accounting is done and maintained by all the nodes rather than controlled by individuals or centralized subjects. Not a single node can tamper the ledger.

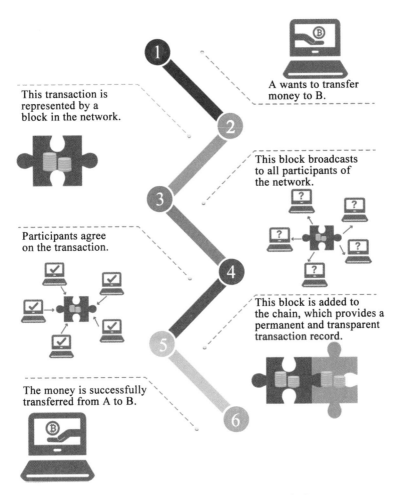

Fig. 2-65: The working process of Blockchain.

If you are going to tamper with a record, you need to control more than 51 percent of the nodes or computing power of the whole network at the same time. It is almost impossible, since there are an infinite amount of nodes, and new ones are added all the time in Blockchain. What is more, the cost of tampering is so high that nearly no one can afford it.

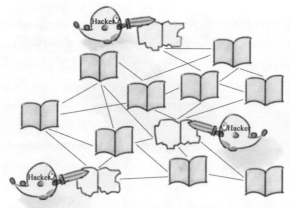

A hacker must control over 51 percent of the nodes of the
network to start an attack, which is difficult to accomplish.

Fig. 2-66: The ledger cannot be compromised.

Four Major Features of Blockchain

After numerous accounting, the Blockchain becomes a reliable public ledger with enormous capacity, which has the following features:

1. **Decentralized:** In a decentralized financial system, there is no intermediary, and all nodes have equal

Decentralization

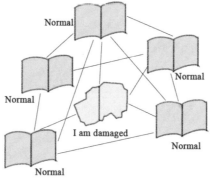

**If a single ledger is damaged, the
system can still proceed normally.**

Fig. 2-67: Features of Blockchain: decentralized.

rights and duties, so that the overall operation of the system will not be affected by the shutdown of any one node.

2. **Detrust:** Thanks to the transparent operation of the database and system, all the nodes can make transactions without issues of trust. Within the rules and time limitations of the system, the nodes cannot deceive one another.

Detrust

Fig. 2-68: Blockchain's characteristics: detrust.

3. **Collectively maintained:** All the nodes have a maintenance function, which means all the users participate in maintaining the system.

Collective maintenance

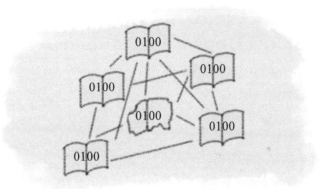

We maintain it together, leaving no one out.

Fig. 2-69: Blockchain's characteristics: collective maintenance.

4. **Reliable database:** Each node in the system has the latest copy of the complete database. It is invalid to modify the database of a single node because the system will automatically make comparisons and take the data most commonly occurring as the real ones.

Reliable database

Fig. 2-70: Features of Blockchain: reliable database.

BLOCKCHAIN'S UNDERLYING STRUCTURE

A Model Framework of Blockchain

The model framework of Blockchain is repeatedly discussed, and people who first get into the industry commonly have questions about its composition. We will demonstrate the framework through the most comprehensive and easiest explanation derived from large amounts of materials. There are six layers of the model framework of Blockchain" data layer, network layer, consensus layer, neuron layer, contract layer, and application layer. Each layer performs a core function, and by cooperating with one another, these layers achieve a decentralized trust mechanism.

A. Data Layer

The data layer mainly represents the physical attributes of Blockchain technology. The first node that the technologists who designed the Blockchain system created was genesis block, then blocks of the same form under the same rules connect together to be a parent Blockchain following a chained structure. As operation duration increases, new blocks are added to the parent Blockchain after being verified, and the parent Blockchain continues to grow longer.

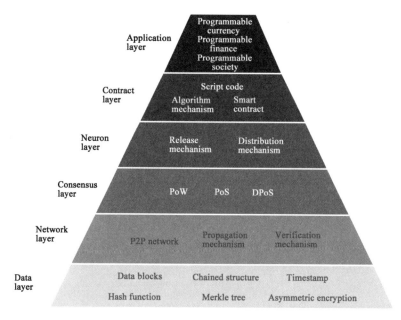

Fig. 2-71: A model framework of Blockchain.

Each block is supported by many technologies such as time-stamping technology, which can ensure that it connects with the other blocks in chronological order, and hash function, which in turn ensures there will be no tampering with that transaction record.

B. Network Layer

The main function of the network layer is to realize the information communication among the nodes in the Blockchain network. Blockchain in nature is a P2P (point to point) network. Every node can both receive and produce information. Nodes achieve communication by jointly maintaining a common Blockchain. Within a Blockchain network, every node can create a new block, and after the creation, it will broadcast to other nodes, which will perform a verification of the new block. With successful verification from over 51 percent of the users within the whole Blockchain network, this new block can be added to the parent Blockchain.

Fig. 2-72: The network layer of Blockchain.

C. Consensus Layer

A consensus layer can help highly dispersed nodes within a decentralized system achieve efficient consensus about the effectiveness of Blockchain data. Common consensus mechanisms in Blockchain include proof-of-work algorithm, proof-of-stake algorithm, and delegated proof-of-stake consensus, which will be the focus in the following chapters.

D. Neuron Layer

The main function of the neuron layer is to provide activation measures, encouraging nodes to participate in the safety verification of Blockchain. Let's take Bitcoin, for example; it has two reward mechanisms. When the number of Bitcoins reaches 21 million, new blocks will no longer generate Bitcoins, at which point the reward mechanism will mainly involve fees that are taken off from every transaction.

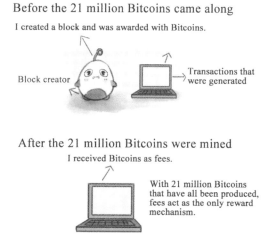

Fig. 2·73: The neuron layer of Blockchain.

E. Contract Layer

The contract layer mainly includes various kinds of script code, algorithm mechanisms, and smart contracts. Let's take Bitcoins, for example: they are programmable currency, and the script code encapsulated in the contract layer stipulates the transaction mode and various details during the transaction process.

F. Application Layer

The application layer encapsulates various application scenarios and cases of Blockchain, such as; OKLink, a cross-border payment platform based on Blockchain, as well as other various applications that we will talk about later in the application chapter.

Basic Types of Blockchain

Public Blockchain

Public Blockchain allows everyone around the world to read, create, acquire verification of transactions, and participate in the consensus process, which decides on the exact blocks that can be added to Blockchain and makes the current status clear.[10]

Public Blockchain

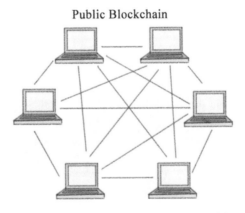

Everyone is given authentication; everyone can participate

Fig. 2-74: Public Blockchain.

Features of Public Blockchain:

1. Protects users from the influence of developers.

   In a public Blockchain, application developers have no right to interfere with users' activities so that the Blockchain can protect its users.

---

10   "A comprehensive introduction to Blockchain: public Blockchain vs private Blockchain" [EB/OL]. (2016–08–09) [2017–05–18]. http://www.weiyangx.com /199778.html.

2. Low access threshold.

All can have the access as long as he or she owns a computer that connects to the internet.

3. All data is open by default.

Every participant in a public Blockchain can access all transaction records in the distributed ledger.

Private Blockchain

Private Blockchain refers to a Blockchain with its writing access belonging to only one organization, aiming to restrict read access and open access.

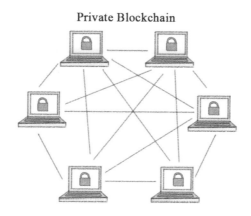

Only an individual or an entity is given authentication.

Fig. 2-75: Private Blockchain.

Features of Private Blockchain:

1. High transaction velocity.

There are fewer nodes in a private Blockchain, and with a high level of trust, not every node is needed to verify a transaction. Thus, the transaction velocity of a private Blockchain is much higher than that of a public Blockchain.

2. Provides better protection for privacy.

   Data in a private Blockchain will not go public and will not be obtained by any individual who has access to the network.

3. Transaction costs can be greatly reduced, even to zero.

   In a private Blockchain, transactions can be achieved free of charge or at least at very low costs. If a physical organization controls and deals with all transactions, then it will no longer need to charge for its operations.

4. Protect basic products from damage.

   By using a private Blockchain, banks and traditional financial organizations can ensure their vested interests and protect their original ecosystem.

Consortium Blockchain

A consortium Blockchain refers to a Blockchain that has its consensus process controlled by preselected nodes. For example, for a consortium Blockchain consisting of fifteen financial organizations, each organization operates a node, and to make every block validated, verification from over half of the consortium, which is eight, is needed. This type of Blockchain may allow everyone to read or can be subjected to participants' hybrid routes.[11]

Consortium Blockchain is regarded as partially decentralized, and the Blockchain project R3 CEV can be seen as a form of consortium Blockchain.

---

11 Huang Butian. "Forms of Blockchain." [EB/OL]. [2017-05-18]. https://wenku .baidu.com/view/ 43d83e1b9ec3d5bbfc0a74be.html.

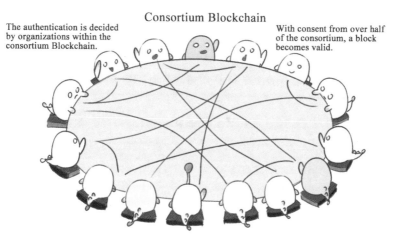

Fig. 2-76: Consortium Blockchain.

Other Classifications

Let's return to other classifications of Blockchain: permission chain, hybrid chain, and complex chain. Permission chain refers to a Blockchain system that requires each node to perform verification. Both private Blockchain and public Blockchain belong to permission chain. With the increasing development of Blockchain technology, its technical framework will not simply consist of private and public Blockchains, and the distinction between the two will be less apparent. Thus, gradually, the concept of complex chain and hybrid chain have been debated.

Development of Blockchain

According to the viewpoints of Melanie Swan, founder of the Institute for Blockchain Studies, there are three stages and fields regarding the development of Blockchain technology: Blockchain 1.0, Blockchain 2.0, and Blockchain 3.0.[12]

---

12 "Blockchain comes, bound to overturn our future life" [EB/OL]. (2016–04–20) [2017–05–18]. http://mt.sohu.com/20160420/n445253975.shtml.

Blockchain 1.0: Programmable currency represented by Bitcoin. It is more like innovation of a digital currency field, such as a system for currency transfer, cashing, and payment.

Blockchain 2.0: Programmable finance based on Blockchain. It is more about innovations in contracts (especially business contracts) and transactions, including stocks, securities, futures, loans, clearing, and settlement, as well as the so-called smart contracts.

Blockchain 3.0: Application of Blockchain in other industries. It refers to changes in man's organizational forms, including health, science, culture, as well as justice and voting based on Blockchain.

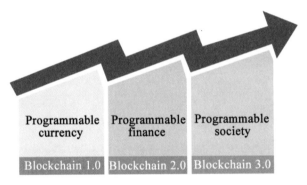

Fig. 2-77: The development of Blockchain.

Consensus Mechanism of Blockchain

Before consensus mechanism, let us take a look at two other introductory problems: the two-army problem and Byzantine failures.

Problem One: The Two-Army Problem

Speaking of this, a popular explanation on the Internet is as follows:

Two armies far apart need to convey information to each other. The blue army sends a messenger to tell the red army: "If you dare, take out the Italian cannons!" Upon receipt of this information, the red army sends a messenger to tell the blue army: "Copy that!" Then the blue army sends a messenger to the red army again: "We know that you have got it." And the red army sends a messenger again: "We know you know we got the information." The blue army sends a messenger again: "We know you know we know you have the information." And then . . . there is no end.

Fig. 2-78: The two-army problem.

Problem Two: Byzantine Failures

This is an old problem, and the details are as follows:

In military actions, The Byzantine Roman Empire decides whether to attack or retreat according to generals' votes. That is to say, if most of the generals decide to attack, the army will rush up. However, if spies are hiding in the army (defecting generals may vote inversely intentionally, or the herald changes the order without authorization), then how to make sure that the result can honestly reflect the will of loyal generals?[13]

Let us explain it further with details.

Long, long ago, a strong empire named Byzantine had extremely powerful armies. There were ten small six of them launched offensives at the same time so that they would have the chance to win, or else they would be defeated. Here comes the problem: in ancient times, communication between armies depended entirely on people. Once there was a spy in a national army, it didn't matter whether it was the general or the signalman who gave the orders; the other

Fig. 2-79: Byzantine failures.

13 Data Sunshine, "On Blockchain from the Technical Perspective" [EB/OL]. (2016–10–17) [2017–05–18]. http://sanwen.net/a/unmoipo.html.

nine countries might receive false information, resulting in failure. If you were the king of one of those small countries, how could you ensure more than five countries would fight alongside you? After all, if you were not careful enough, you might lose the country.

These problems are why we need to reach consensus. There are various consensus mechanisms in Blockchain. None of them is perfect, so none of them can be applied to all scenarios. Below, we will go over different consensus mechanisms discussed by Mr. Zhang in his article "Consensus mechanism on blockchain." We selected nine kinds of consensus mechanisms with comparatively specific features to make a brief introduction. The common consensus mechanisms include nine types, including, most significantly, Proof of Work, Proof of State, and Delegated Proof of Stake.

A: PROOF OF WORK

Proof of Work (PoW) can usually only be proved from the results because monitoring the work process is cumbersome and inefficient.

When Bitcoin generates blocks, PoW is employed. The hash of a matching block consists of N preleading zeros. The number of zeros depends on the difficulty of the network. To get a reasonable block hash value requires a lot of tests and calculations, and the calculation time depends on the machine's hash operation speed. When a node provides a reasonable block hash value, it indicates that the node has indeed gone through a large number of calculations; of course, this does not give the absolute number of calculations, because finding a reasonable hash value is a probabilistic event. When a node occupies a computing power of n percent of the entire network, then the node has a n percent probability of finding the block hash.

PoW relies on machines to conduct mathematical operations and then obtain the right to record. The operations consume immense resources and have high consensus mechanism and weak supervision. Meanwhile, each consensus needs the whole network to participate in calculating and has a relatively low efficiency and performance ratio, as well as a fault-tolerance of allowing 50 percent of the nodes in the entire Internet to be in error.

Advantages of PoW: Completely decentralized; free access to nodes.

Disadvantages of PoW: Currently, Bitcoin has attracted most of the global computing power; other Blockchain applications using the PoW consensus can hardly obtain the same computing power to protect their own security. Also, mining causes much waste of resources, and the time to reach consensus is relatively long.

The projects using PoW: Bitcoin, the first three stages of Ethereum—Frontier, Homestead, and Metropolis. The fourth stage of Ethereum, Serenity, will use the PoS.

B. Proof of Stake

Proof of Stake (PoS) was first proposed by the "Quantum Mechanic" at the 2011 Bitcoin Forum's Lecture and was later implemented by Peercoin (DOT) and NXT (Futures) with different ideas.

The main idea of PoS is that the difficulty of acquiring recording rights for nodes is inversely proportional to the rights and benefits held by nodes. Compared with PoW, it reduces certain resource consumption caused by mathematical operations.

The performance has been correspondingly improved. But based on hashing, the regulation on competing for the recording right is still weak. The fault tolerance of PoS is the same as PoW. It is an upgrade of PoW, which reduces the difficulty of mining in proportion to time and to tokens occupied by each node and thus speeds up the process of finding random numbers.

In PoW, a user may use $1,000 to buy a computer, join the network to mine, create a new block, and then get rewarded. In the PoS, users can purchase equivalent tokens for $1,000 and put these tokens as deposits into the PoS mechanism. Users thereby have the chance to create new blocks and get rewards.

Random selection of PoS algorithm

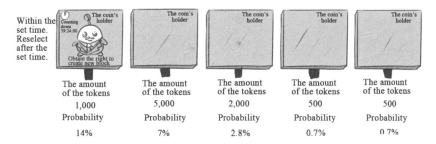

Fig. 2-80: PoS Random Selected Algorithm.

In general, there is a collection of coin holders in this system. Holders put tokens into the PoS mechanism, and then they become verifiers. For the first block in Blockchain, the PoS algorithm randomly selects one among the verifiers (the verifier's weight is based on the number of tokens they invest). For example, the chance for a verifier investing 10,000 tokens is 10 times as that of the one investing 1,000 tokens, which gives him the right to create the next block. Within a certain time, if the verifier has not yet generated a block, a second verifier is instead selected to generate a new block. Like PoW, PoS chooses the longest link.

With economies of scale (referring to the phenomenon of increasing economic efficiency due to the expansion of production scale) disappearing, the risk of centralization is reduced. The tokens worth $10 million bring a return that is exactly 10 times the value of tokens worth of $1 million, and no one will receive disproportional additional rewards for the ability to afford large-scale production tools.

Advantages of PoS: It somehow shortens the time for reaching consensus and no longer needs to consume enormous energy to mine.

Disadvantages of PoS: Mining is still needed without eradicating the deadly flaw in commercial applications, and any confirmation is only probabilistic rather than deterministic. Theoretically, there may be other attacks, for example, Ethereum's DAO attack causing Ethereum to fork and the ETC to appear, which in fact proved the failure of this hard fork.

C. DELEGATED PROOF OF STATE

The BitShares community first raised the idea of the DPoS mechanism. The main difference between DPoS and PoS is that the node elects several delegates, who verify and record transactions, but its compliance and supervision, performance, resource consumption, and fault tolerance are similar to those of PoS. Similar to board voting, the token holders elect and entrust a certain number of nodes to verify and record transactions.

The working principle of DPoS is as follows: Each shareholder has a corresponding influence in proportion to his percentages of shareholding, and the result of 51 percent of shareholder voting will be irreversible and binding. The challenge is to achieve "51 percent approval" in a timely and efficient method. To achieve this goal, each shareholder can entrust his vote to a delegate. The top 100 delegates with the most votes generate blocks according to the established schedule. Each delegate is assigned to a certain time to generate a block.

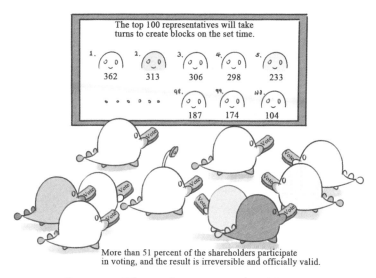

Fig. 2-81: The working principle of DPoS.

All delegates will receive 10 percent of the transaction fee that is equivalent to an average block. If an average block takes 100 shares as a transaction fee, one delegate can receive one share as the reward.

Some delegates may fail to broadcast their blocks promptly due to the network latency, which will result in a fork in Blockchain. However, this is unlikely to happen, because the delegate who generates the block can establish a direct connection with the delegates of the block before and after. Establishing this direct connection with the delegate behind you (and possibly the one after you) will ensure that you get paid.

Under the DPoS's voting mode, a new block can be generated every thirty seconds. In normal network conditions, the possibility of a fork in Blockchain is extremely small, and even if it happens, it can be resolved in a few minutes.

The basic steps to perform this mode are:

1. **Become a delegate.** To become a delegate, you must register your public key on the Internet and get a 32-bit unique identifier. This identifier is quoted by the "head" of each transaction's data.

2. **Keep the nodes honest.** There will be a monitoring service in the system, which will calculate the behavior of each node in real time, which is equivalent to an automated error correction mechanism. Let me give an example. If a node does not produce a new block as expected, then it is considered that this node automatically gives up its right to produce the block, so the next node generates a new block.

3. **Delegates represent integrity.** Each wallet will display a status indicator to let users know how their delegates perform. If they miss too many blocks, the system will recommend that the user replace them with new ones. If any delegate is found to have issued an invalid block, then all standard wallets will ask to select a new delegate before each wallet makes further transactions.

4. **Attack resistance.** For attack resistance, the power obtained by the top 100 delegates is the same, namely, each delegate has an equal voting right. Thus, it is impossible to obtain more than 1 percent of the votes and concentrate the power on a single delegate. With only 100 delegates, it is not difficult to imagine an attacker who could perform "denial of service" attacks on the delegates whose turn is to generate the block. Fortunately, because the identity of each delegate is the public key instead of the IP address, the threat of this particular attack can be easily mitigated. This will make it more difficult to determine the attack target of DDoS (Distributed Denial of Service). The potential connections between delegates will make it more difficult to hinder the block-generating process.

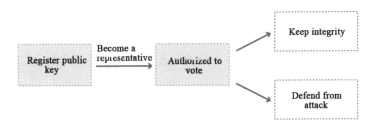

Certificate of equity authorization

Fig. 2-82: The voting pattern of DPoS.

Advantages of DPoS: The number of nodes participating in verification and recording is significantly reduced, and second-level consensus verification is achieved.

Disadvantages of DPoS: The entire consensus mechanism relies on tokens, but many commercial applications do not require tokens.

D. BETTING CONSENSUS

Betting Consensus is a brand-new concept introduced by the consensus mechanism of next-generation Ethereum Casper, which belongs to PoS. Casper's consensus is reached based on blocks instead of chains like PoS.

To prevent verifiers from offering different bets in different fields, we have another simple but strict rule: if you bet the same numbers twice, or you submit a bet that Casper can't process according to the protocol, you will lose all your deposits. This is how Casper differs from a traditional PoS punishment system. In this way, illegal nodes maliciously attacking can't get transaction fees and will risk having their deposits confiscated.

The verifiers of Casper protocol should complete two activities: block generating and betting:

Block generating is a process independent from other events. Verifiers collect transactions, and when it's their turn to generate a block, they generate the block, sign, and send it to the network. The betting is more complicated. Currently, Casper's default verifier strategy is designed to imitate the Byzantine Fault Tolerance, to observe how other verifiers bet, take the value at the 33 percent point, and move a step farther to 0 or 1.

The client verifies the current situation with the following process: First, they download all the blocks and bets, then opinions are formed using the algorithm mentioned above but not published; they simply observe different heights in the sequence. If the chance of one block is over 0.5, they process it. Otherwise, they skip it. The situation after all blocks are processed is displayed as the "current situation." The client can also give some objective opinions on the "final verification."

If the opinion by all blocks before height k is over 99.999 percent or below 0.0001 percent, the client can see that the first k clients are finally verified.

E. Ripple Consensus

The Ripple Consensus algorithm enables a group of nodes to reach a consensus based on a special list of initial nodes. The special list of initial nodes is like a club. To accept a new member, 51 percent of the members of the club must pass it. The consensus follows the "51 percent power" of these core members, and outsiders have no influence. Since the club starts from centralization, it will always be centralized, and if it starts to corrupt, shareholders can do nothing. Like Bitcoin and Peercoin, the Ripple system separates shareholders from their voting rights, so it is more centralized than other systems.

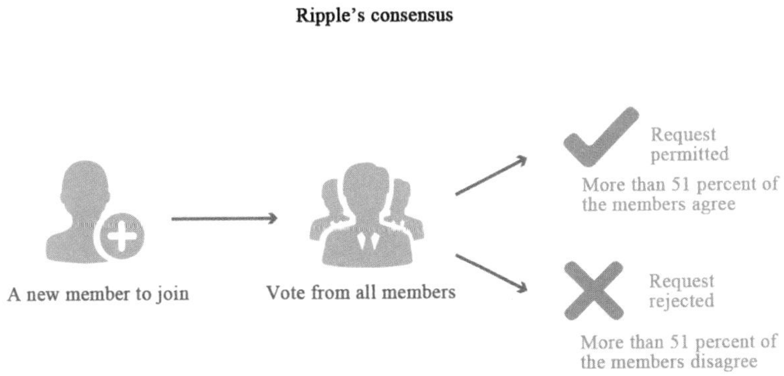

Ripple's consensus

A new member to join   Vote from all members

Request permitted
More than 51 percent of the members agree

Request rejected
More than 51 percent of the members disagree

Fig. 2-83: Ripple Consensus.

F. Pool

Based on the traditional distributed consistency technique and data verification mechanism, Pool is the consensus mechanism widely used in the Bitcoin industry today. Its pros and cons are as follows:

Advantages: It can work without tokens. Based on sophisticated distributed consistency algorithm (Pasox, Raft, etc.), it can achieve second-level consensus verification.

Disadvantages: The level of decentralization is weaker than Bitcoin and is more suitable for a centralized business pattern with various participants.

G. PRACTICAL BYZANTINE FAULT TOLERANCE

For distributed calculation, different computers try to reach consensus by exchanging information. Sometimes, the coordinator or some members in the system may exchange incorrect information due to system error. For a Byzantine Generals Problem, based on the numbers of the computers in error, there won't be definite answers for a possible resolution, but there will be ways to verify the efficiency of a mechanism.

Fig. 2-84: Byzantine Fault Tolerance.

The possible resolution: under the condition of $N \geq 3F + 1$, consistency is achievable (N is the total number of computers; F is the total number of fault computers). After information is exchanged between computers, each computer lists all the information it gets, then the result obtained by most computers is taken as the resolution.

Practical Byzantine Fault Tolerance (PBFT) was created by Castro and Liskov in 1999 and is the first widely applied Byzantine Fault Tolerance Algorithm. If 2/3 of the nodes in the system function normally, the consistency can be ensured.

The overall process of the practical Byzantine Fault Tolerance algorithm is as follows: The client sends a request to the masternode to invoke a service operation, such as "<REQUEST, o, t, c>," where client c requests to execute operation o, and the timestamp t is used to guarantee the client's request will only be executed once. Each message sent from the replica node to the client contains the current view number for the client to trace, so the current masternode number can be further deduced. The client sends a request to its own masternode via a P2P message, and then the masternode automatically broadcasts the request to all backup nodes.

View numbers are consecutively numbered integers. The masternode is calculated by the formula $p = v \mod |R|$, where v is the view number, p is the copy number, and $|R|$ is the number of replica sets.

The response from the replica to the client is "<REPLY,v,t,c,i,r>," where v is the view number, t is the timestamp, i is the number of the replica, and r is the result of the request execution.

The masternode broadcasts the request to other replicas and then begins performing tasks in three stages:

1. **Prepreparation stage.** The masternode assigns a sequence number, n, to the received request and then sends a preprepared message to all backup nodes. The format of the prepared message is "<<PRE-PRE-PARE,v,n,d>,m>," where v is the view number, m is the request message sent by the client, and d is the summary of the request message m.

2. **Preparation stage.** If backup node i accepts the preprepared message, it enters the preparation stage. While preparing, the node sends a preparation message "<PREPARE,v,n,d,i>" to all replica nodes and writes the preprepared message and the preparation message in its own log.

3. **Confirmation stage.** When the "(m, v, n, i)" condition is true, replica i broadcasts "<COM-MIT, v, n, D(m), i>" to other replica nodes and then enters the confirmation stage. All replicas execute the request and send the result back to the client. The client needs to wait for different replicas to send back the same result as the final result of the entire operation.

If the client does not receive a reply by a certain time, the request will be broadcast to all replica nodes; if the request has already been processed at the replica node, the replica will resend the execution result to the client. If the request is not processed at the replica node, the replica node will forward the request to the masternode; if the masternode does not broadcast the request, then it is considered to be invalid. If there are enough replica nodes that think the masternode fails, a view change will be triggered.

Figure 2-85 displays the normal execution process of the algorithm when an invalid masternode does not exist. In the figure, 0 is the masternode, replica 3 is the invalid node, and c is the client:

The following chart illustrates the execution flow of algorithms when main nodes are valid. Copy 0 is main node, copy 3 is invalid node, and copy C is client.

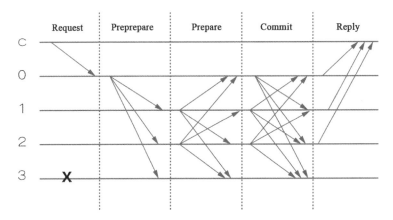

Fig. 2-85: The algorithm when a masternode is valid.

The practical Byzantine Fault Tolerance is a consensus mechanism that adopts "permitted voting and minority subordination" to elect leaders and keep books. This consensus mechanism allows Byzantine Fault Tolerance and the participation of strong supervisory nodes and has authority rating capability, higher performance, and lower energy consumption. During each round of voting, nodes in the entire network elect the leaders, allowing 33 percent of the nodes to do evil, namely, 33 percent fault tolerance. Because it is suitable for the application scenario of the consortium Blockchain, the Practical Byzantine Fault Tolerance mechanism and its improved algorithm are currently the most widely used consensus algorithms for consortium Blockchain. The improved algorithm is optimized in the following ways: it modifies the requirements of the underlying network topology and uses P2P networks, it can adjust the number of nodes, and it reduces the number of messages used by the protocol.

H. Delegated Byzantine Fault Tolerance

In April 2016, Antshares released a consensus algorithm white paper, describing a universal consensus mechanism—Delegated Byzantine Fault Tolerance—and proposing an improved Byzantine Fault Tolerance algorithm that can be applied to Blockchain systems. Based on the Practical Byzantine Fault Tolerance algorithm, the Delegated Byzantine Fault Tolerance algorithm offers the following improvements:

1. Improves the request response pattern of the C/S (client/server) to the P2P network-suited equal nodes pattern.
2. Improves the static node participating in consensus into a consensus participation node that can access and withdraw dynamically.
3. Designs and generates a voting system for nodes participating in consensus based on the proportion of equity ownership and decides the nodes participating in consensus by voting.
4. Introduces the digital certificates in Blockchain and solves the problem of verifying the accounting node's authentic identity during the voting.

Advantages of DBFT: Has professionalized bookkeepers, tolerance to any types of faults, multipeople cooperative book-keeping, finality of each block, no forks, and reliable algorithm with strict mathematical proof.

Disadvantages of DBFT: When 1/3 or more of the book-keepers stop working, the system will be unable to provide services. When 1/3 or more of the bookkeepers commit a crime, and the other bookkeepers are segmented into two Internet islands, the criminal bookkeepers can utilize the forks in the system, but leave cryptographic evidence.

To sum up, the core of DBFT ensures the system's finality to the maximum extent and makes Blockchain suitable for real-world financial applications.

I. Paxos Algorithm

Paxos Algorithm is a traditional distributed consistency algo-rithm. It's a consensus mechanism based on leader election: it has leader nodes with absolute authority, the participation of strong regulation nodes, high performance, and low resource consumption. All nodes usually have offline accessing mech-anisms, but malicious nodes are not allowed during the elec-tion, so there is no fault tolerance.

3.

THE PEOPLE

They made history.

With good prospects in the 21st century, the Blockchain industry sees its talents appearing successively, each playing a long-term, leading role. In this chapter, I have selected a few characters and representative personages to tell the stories about people in this industry.

Of course, many of us have debated the selection extensively. From the initial twenty to the final five people, we've had countless discussions. In the end, I have chosen to explore those who may not be the most famous but are relatively distinct.

One is a legend we cannot ignore: Satoshi Nakamoto. One is a forerunner and pioneer in the field of Blockchain technology, Nick Szabo, who proposed smart contracts. Then we have two distinctive opinion leaders: Marc Andreessen, a Bitcoin columnist for the *New York Times*; and Blythe Masters, an extraordinary woman from Wall Street. Finally, there is Barry Silbert, a tycoon investing in the Blockchain industry.

ETERNAL LEGEND: 99 SPECULATIONS ABOUT SATOSHI NAKAMOTO

Considering legendary figures in the Blockchain industry, we will always start with Satoshi Nakamoto, the designer of Bitcoin and even the creator of the core theory of Blockchain. Let's make a slightly exaggerated metaphor: When God created the world, he said, "Let there be light," and there was light; whereas when Satoshi was typing at the computer, he shouted, "Come on, my Bitcoin," and there was Bitcoin as well as the Blockchain technology behind.

Fig. 3-1: Satoshi Nakamoto.

This legend is about a man who is not only very talented, but also very interesting. Obviously, Satoshi could gain both fame and fortune depending on his talent, but he deliberately avoids that, turning into quite a character and a thorough mystery. When Bitcoin was first developed, Satoshi participated as an anonymous guide, and as Bitcoin and Blockchain gained more and more popularity, however, he disappeared completely. He uses none of his Bitcoins with the total value of several billion US dollars, nor does he apply for any patent, and he never shows up—even when nominated for the Nobel Prize in economics.

Fig. 3-2: Nominees for Nobel Prize in economics.

Whoever he is, when he will appear, and whether he will show up in his life, there is no doubt that he has realized dreams many have harbored since childhood—"I want to change the world," and "I want to be the mystery of the world." Here, we will intricately explore the legendary experience of this talent.

Satoshi is portrayed as an economist, mathematician, cryptologist, and top hacker in people's minds. His legendary history began on November 1, 2008, when he published a paper "Bitcoin: A Peer-to-Peer Electronic Cash System." He then put the theory into practice, creating the first block of the Bitcoin world on January 4, 2009, which we call Genesis Block. In the same year on January 11, he released a client with a very simple name—the Version 0.1 of Bitcoin, summoning every like-minded person.

The story evolves slowly: the first deal in Bitcoin was completed, the Bitcoin exchange rate was first calculated, chat rooms were ready for Bitcoin tech lovers, and the Bitcoin mining difficulty got adjusted. For the first time, several countries, such as Germany and Malta, began implementing laws that recognized Bitcoin, and its market value reached nearly 40 billion US dollars (estimates according to data in May 2017). Of course, the growth of Bitcoin is also accompanied by some "negative energy," such as its price soaring and plummeting and its involvement in theft or lawsuit. In short, Bitcoin has a rich and colorful history, and we will elaborate on it later.

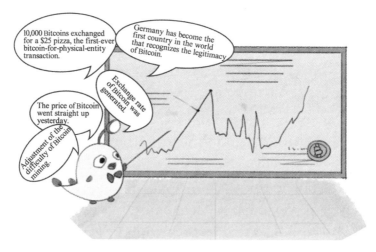

Fig. 3-3: The rich and colorful Bitcoin history.

What role did Satoshi play in these events? He was a creator. The FBI and all the media around the world are looking for him, but in vain. Everyone can find his words in the forums, his e-mails, and his website homepage posted during the initial creation of Bitcoin in 2008, but all the inquiries into these ostensible clues resulted in a dead end.

Fig. 3-4: The world is looking for Satoshi Nakamoto.

Several significant events in Bitcoin history have been caused by the name "Satoshi." For example, shortly after a Japanese man was recognized as Satoshi, some people decided he was Australian, and then the *New York Times* claimed to have found the real Satoshi. A recent sensation was brought about by Australian entrepreneur Craig Stephen Wright, who declared himself the real Satoshi Nakamoto. On the BBC, and in *The Economist* and GQ, he showed a deal made in January

Fig. 3-5: Mystery of Satoshi's identity.

2009 by Satoshi transferring 10 Bitcoins to Harry Finney, one of the programmers who helped build the Bitcoin protocol. This deal was the first-ever transfer transaction within the Bitcoin system. At the same time, he also submitted over fifty patent applications to Britain involving Bitcoin and its underlying Blockchain technology.

Everyone thought Satoshi was found, so one after another, they hurried to besiege him, looking for a scoop. *Wired* stirred the pot forty-eight hours later by publishing articles about the situation. Finally, the wave was calmed by Satoshi's e-mail, in which he said with a sense of detachment: "I am not Craig Wright. We are all Satoshi."

Actually, it is simple to prove the identity of Satoshi, because Bitcoin is a distributed ledger in nature. That is, it is a ledger that cannot be modified, destroyed, or interrupted, and everyone can gain access to it. Therefore, how does one authenticate his identity based on the distributed ledger? First, he can publish a Bitcoin public key to announce that he has the private key corresponding to this public key; then, if he can sign a message with this private key, his words are demonstrated.

So, how can one prove that he is Satoshi? Just use the private key to the Genesis block to sign a message, whatever the message is, and if the signature gets authenticated by the corresponding public key, he is Satoshi—because the private key to Genesis block must belong to the creator of Bitcoin.[14]

Nowadays, the market value of Bitcoin has drastically outpaced that of legal tender in many countries. Quite a lot of

---

14 "Who on earth is Satoshi Nakamoto and what is Bitcoin's private key technology?" [EB/OL]. (2016-07-15) [2017-05-18]. http://zhuanlan.zhihu.com/p /21722963.

governments have ratified its legal status or eased restrictions on it, and Blockchain applications have flourished everywhere as a hot "upstart" in the financial technology field. It is estimated that Satoshi Nakamoto holds about 1 million Bitcoins as well as countless patents. He is the ultimate successful legend. There was no shortage of people who wanted to create a currency on their own in history, but only Satoshi Nakamoto did so.

As Satoshi himself said, "Everyone can be Satoshi," because we all can be practitioners of Blockchain technology. And we all look forward to embracing a new world revolutionized by Blockchain.

Satoshi often appears mysteriously in illustrations, and we can see nothing but his blurry profile. However, "Everyone can be Satoshi," and we are ready to witness the new legends created by each Satoshi.

WHEN NICK SZABO WAS "HIT" BY VENDING MACHINES

Just like Newton was hit in the head with a falling "God's apple" from the tree and then came up with the laws of motion, there is also a person in the Blockchain field "hit" by vending machines, enabling him to propose the concept of "smart contract." Vending machines are familiar to us, and these clumsy machines are very "smart," as products are released once money is inserted into the machine. Although we have no idea about its internal working mechanism, it is common sense to us that a vending machine can provide various items after money is inserted. The person inspired by vending machines and who first conceptualized smart contract is Nick Szabo, a computer scientist, cryptographer, legal scholar, and inventor, of the concept of a smart contract. Some even believe that Nick Szabo is probably Satoshi Nakamoto. He is now raising funds to launch a Blockchain technology company.

Fig. 3-6: Nick Szabo.

The best way to introduce a scientist is to narrate his inventions. In the eye of Nick Szabo, vending machines take on a unique glamour, as when consumers insert money into them and select items they want to buy, an enforceable contract will be launched between consumers and vending machines. Buyers insert money into the machine and choose items, while sellers are responsible for providing products and small change through the internal logic of vending machines.

Fig. 3-7: The logic of vending machines.

If a vending machine fails to provide items after payment has been tendered, people think that the machine does not abide by the prescriptive contract, and some even become angry and kick the machine. However, the machine is actually

Fig. 3-8: Simple smart contracts.

very innocent. It may fail to identify coins because previous customers have inserted counterfeit money, so the machine has reason to refuse to release products. This is a kind of simplified smart contract.

A question from *Quirkology* is another example: What to do if you have paid the money for items bought online, but the seller lies and claims that he has delivered goods that he hasn't? How do these two parties resolve their case? Alipay, serving as the third party, can avoid such issues in a transaction, because the buyer's payment for items will first be sent into Alipay, and only after the seller has delivered the items to the buyer will Alipay send him the payment. This way, the interests of two parties in a transaction are protected. It's known as the model of secured transactions. Alipay, although it is a kind of payment tool, almost shares the same working mechanism with smart contract—based on trust. However, Alipay is also faced with a potential threat. If unidentified objects intrude on its server, it could lead the whole system into a breakdown and eliminate all transaction records. The buyer and the seller would then be unable to resolve their transactions.

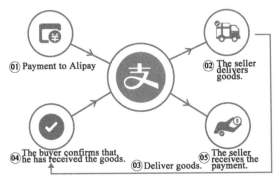

Fig. 3-9: The logic of Alipay.

The definition of a smart contract is a computer program and a decentralized system that is available to all users without intermediaries. It has the following prerequisites:

1. Currency is a must, whether it is a legal currency or an encrypted digital currency, because there is no so-called transaction without currencies.

2. Assets must be digitalized. However, how can a car be digitalized? The answer is to equip it with a cryptography lock. Since cars are still equipped with physical locks, the delivery of cars is actually the delivery of car keys to their owners. Imagine that in the future, the public key of cryptography can be used as keys, and only the person with a private key has access to the car. It's miraculous, isn't it? But this fantasy can be turned into reality.

3. Assets must be connected to the Internet and must entirely trust a particular database.

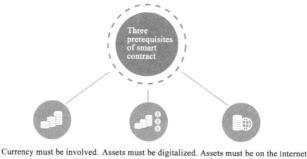

Currency must be involved. Assets must be digitalized. Assets must be on the Internet and trust a certain database.

Fig. 3-10: Characteristics of smart contracts.

Essentially, smart contracts are very similar to an "if . . . then" statement in other computer programs regarding working principles and interaction with assets in the real world.

When a preset condition is triggered, smart contracts will implement the corresponding clauses in contracts.[15] At present, Union Bank of Switzerland, Barclays in England, JPMorgan in the US, and other financial institutions are studying how to apply smart contracts to automated clearing systems, which has the potential to reduce costs sharply.

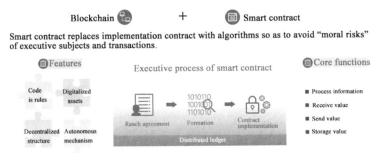

Fig. 3-11: A structural model of smart contracts.

Once the above three conditions are achieved, smart contracts will operate like today's Alipay, and customers trust and use it to complete transactions without the need to know the technology behind it. Smart contracts will become ubiquitous in the world of Blockchain.

FEMALE LEADERS WITH WALL STREET BACKGROUNDS IN THE BLOCKCHAIN COMMUNITY

As Bitcoin and Blockchain technology often have an air of mystique and those who know little about them are often left shrouded in confusion, authorities and opinion leaders in the Blockchain community are mostly low-profile men who are

---

15 "Smart contracts will enable us to be free from banks and lawyers in the future" EB/OL]. (2016-06-21) [2017-05-18]. http://it.sohu.com/20160621/n455402402 .shtml.

stingy with their views. However, there are some outstanding female opinion leaders attracting our attention, like Catherine Nicholson, CEO of the Blockchain startup BlockCypher that has raised US$3.5 million; and Blythe Masters, CEO of Digital Asset Holdings.

Fig. 3-12: Catherine Nicholson.

Blythe Masters is a former senior executive of JPMorgan, where she worked for almost thirty years. She is now the founder and CEO of Digital Asset Holdings, a startup aiming to spread Blockchain technology to Wall Street.

Currently, Digital Asset Holdings is working together with Ms. Masters's previous employer, JPMorgan (also its first big client), to speed up the settlement through testing Blockchain technology. As Babbitt writes, "Blockchain technology will be deployed in business environment in various forms. However, it doesn't mean that it will become the mainstream. I think it still takes five to ten years for Blockchain to be the

Fig. 3-13: Female opinion leaders in the Blockchain community.

mainstream."[16] Digital Asset Holdings is the recipient of US$60 million in financing. Masters's backing, as she enjoys enormous popularity on Wall Street, may enable Blockchain technology to exert a positive influence on the traditional financial industry.

THE MAN WRITING COLUMNS FOR THE *NEW YORK TIMES*

In 1971, a young boy was born in Iowa, and at that time, no one saw that he would change the world's communication pattern when he grew up. He learned to use a computer when he was nine and began teaching himself BASIC programming

---

16 Babbitt. "CEO of Digital Asset Holdings: Blockchain technology will be applied to banks in two years but it still takes five to ten years for this technology to become mainstream." [EB/OL]. (2016–04–07) [2017–05–18]. http://www.8btc .com/ Blockchain-in-banks-a-reality.

language (Beginners' All-purpose Symbolic Instruction Code) from a library book at the same age. Hailed as a precursor to the Internet, he also dared to challenge Warren Buffett, claiming, "Bitcoin is like the technology from Mars." He is the fourth figure we will mention in this chapter—Marc Andreessen, the columnist who writes articles concerning Bitcoin for the *New York Times.*

Fig. 3-14: Marc Andreessen.

Fig. 3-15: Teaching himself BASIC language when he was a child.

A brief introduction to this accomplished legend may help you understand him. Marc Andreessen, though not as famous as Bill Gates and Steve Jobs, still exerts significant influence on the development of the Internet with his achievements. Now, let's begin with his entrepreneurial experiences.

In the first decade of his career, Andreessen founded Netscape, the first web browser. In 1992, Andreessen worked with his partners to develop the first graphical web browser, Mosaic, and launched Netscape with his partners a year later. In 1995, Netscape went public in New York with a market capitalization of US$2.9 billion, enabling this twenty-four-year-old entrepreneur to become a billionaire overnight. However, his first entrepreneurial experience came to an end in 1999 with the rise of the IE browser, the web browser of Microsoft, which forced Netscape to be acquired by America Online.

Andreessen's second entrepreneurial experience also involved the Internet. He went on to found a cloud computing company named Loudcloud with his partners. Nevertheless, the Internet bubble, burst during 2002–2006, deprived venture capital firms of the willingness to invest in Internet companies, which led this firm to be acquired by HP for US $1.6 billion in 2007.

Later, Andreessen joined the board of directors of Facebook and served as a consultant for Evan Williams, who was then the CEO of Twitter. In 2009, Andreessen launched Andreessen Horowitz with Ben Horowitz.

Andreessen Horowitz formed Marc Andreessen's indissoluble bond with Bitcoin, as they invested in Coinbase, a Bitcoin trading system; 21Inc, a Bitcoin start-up, and TradeBlock, a Blockchain data provider. Of course, these accomplishments alone aren't what justifies his selection as an influential figure in the Blockchain field.

Fig. 3-16: Andreessen Horowitz.

In the Blockchain industry, Marc Andreessen is famous for his opinions and explosive remarks, which often attract media reprint. In 2014, he began to write columns for the

Fig. 3-17: Columnist of the *New York Times*.

New York Times, and his first article used a bold title—"Why Bitcoin Matters." Apart from that, he also heartily shares news concerning Bitcoin and Blockchain with his fans on Twitter.

In 2014, investment guru Warren Buffett warned that Bitcoin was basically a mirage and that investors should stay away from it. Marc Andreessen responded, "old white men crapping on new technology they don't understand." International media covered the feud. When interviewed, Andreessen said, "Bitcoin is like the technology from Mars." At the same time, he also actively shared his views about Bitcoin and Blockchain technology during many of the interviews.

Fig. 3-18: "Against" Buffett.

Arguably, Marc Andreessen is a bold and courageous opinion leader and has made contributions to popularize Bitcoin and Blockchain technology internationally.

A Big Fish Who Wants to Invest in All Digital Currencies

Let's move to next story about a "strange" person who started an adventurous journey in the business world with his unique approach—"buy, buy, buy." Now and then, we learn online that xx Blockchain company is sold, xx Bitcoin company is acquired, or xx FinTech firm is invested. However, what we do not know is that the same person is always behind this news, that is, Barry Silbert, CEO of Digital Currency Group.

Fig. 3-19: Barry Silbert.

Silbert's "acquisition list" involves about twenty countries across the world, and he has invested in up to sixty companies. DCG was launched by Barry Silbert, and it is structured as an investment company rather than an investment fund.

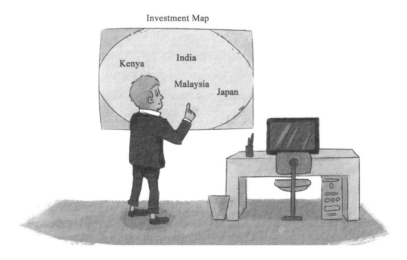

Fig. 3-20: Global investment profile.

"DCG provides the flexibility to invest in companies, buy companies and hold permanent capital. So the money that we raise stays within the company; instead of having a fund where you have to return capital to your limited partners, we get to deploy capital within our company. . . . Our mission is to accelerate the development of a better financial system," he said.[17]

DCG is deeply fond of Blockchain, and it mainly invests in Bitcoin-based startups. Its early investments included Ripple, the first network in the world that allows all customers to do transactions; Coinbase; and BitPay, a Bitcoin payment service provider. At the same time, DCG also invested in fifteen exchanges around the world, including Unocoin in India, Korbit in Korea, BitFlyer in Japan, BitPesa in Kenya, and BitXin Malaysia, which supports up to forty different currency pairs. It recently invested in Skuchain, a Blockchain company that optimizes supply chains by utilizing Blockchain technology. Apart from the "buy, buy, buy" strategy, Barry Silbert is one of the few investors out there who is excited about Bitcoin as a currency. He once remarked that "Brexit shows how Bitcoin shines as a safe-haven asset."

Regarding traditional financial magnates' enthusiasm toward Blockchain technology, he said, "We are excited about the fact that Blockchain technology is deployed in financial institutions, whether it is Bitcoin's Blockchain or not. But we still focus on building Bitcoin into a global currency, this is our vision."

---

17 "Barry Silbert talked about DCG's investment strategies in digital currency field." (2016–02–01) [2017–05–18]. http://www.okcoin.cn/t-1010622.html.

The examples above show that Barry Silbert is a "pious believer" of Bitcoin and Blockchain technology, and he has been practicing his firm faith with his unique strategy—"continuous buy-in."

Fig. 3-21: Believer in Bitcoin.

4.

THE APPLICATION

Ten years later, let's enjoy the boom of Blockchain.

Maybe it was through Bitcoin or a financial technology summit that you first heard of Blockchain. But nowadays, almost all sectors claim that they have something to do with Blockchain.

We are actively exploring Blockchain technology; we are launching Blockchain labs, we boast about an expert and also a "big fish" in the Blockchain industry who will lead us to explore the new transformation path of our company with Blockchain technology: such statements are heard almost everywhere. It seems that everything in the world can be connected to Blockchain. However, is it fact or just a hot topic?

In this chapter, we are going to share "Blockchain plus" with you by choosing several popular fields and related cases to demonstrate how this technology exerts influence on different fields. I will then cite many real examples at home and abroad, as well as the opinions of experts. Pertinent references and their sources will be annotated in the last part of this book.

FINANCE

Nowadays, Blockchain, as a phenomenal concept, has received recognition from governments, companies, and institutions, but do you have any idea about which industry first witnessed its boom? Yes, it was the financial industry. Although the application of Blockchain in the financial sector is not mature enough, and there is no financial magnate who can match Baidu, Alibaba, and Tencent, one thing we know for sure is that Blockchain will undoubtedly have a disruptive influence on the traditional financial industry as an increasing number of large financial institutions are beginning to conduct Blockchain experiments and attain gradual achievements. It is even expected that Blockchain, like big data and artificial intelligence, can serve as a key to opening the door to the new era of Internet finance.

Over the past two years, more than twenty top global financial institutions including JP Morgan, Goldman Sachs Group, and Citibank have invested more than US$1 billion in Blockchain projects. It is estimated that in 2017, the investment in Blockchain will only be more, and it may exceed one billion US dollars in only one year.

BANKS

In the current banking systems of most countries, all banks check their accounts through an electronic ledger, a centralized structure that has more authorities and larger stored data volume as the institution approaches closer to the central part of this structure. At the same time, they need to spend extensively on cooperation costs to maintain data accuracy in this decentralized system. Since Blockchain technology is decentralized, it can create a distributed and open network for banks, in which all transaction data will be transparent and shared by everyone. Distributed accounting based on Blockchain technology has the ability to remove invalid bank intermediaries and cut operating costs significantly.

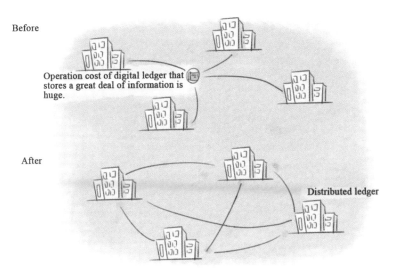

Fig. 4-1: Blockchain plus banks.

At present, Blockchain technology has received recognition from many banks that have launched Blockchain labs, in which they are devoted to developing tools to transform the whole banking system. According to a report from Spain, US$15 to US$22 billion in operating costs are expected to be saved every year before 2022 if Blockchain technology is applied to banks.

The mainstream and traditional cross border remittance is a wire transfer, in which funds may take three to five workdays to move from the remitter's account to the receiver's account. Besides, bank intermediaries and Society Worldwide Interbank Financial Telecommunication (SWIFT) charge communication fees toward message exchanges through their system. For example, in China, 150 yuan will be charged as the telecommunication fee by Bank of China when a cross border transfer is made.

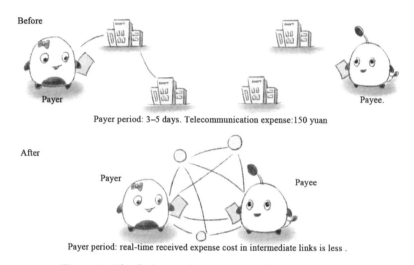

Payer period: 3–5 days. Telecommunication expense:150 yuan

Payer period: real-time received expense cost in intermediate links is less .

Fig. 4-2: Blockchain plus cross border payments.

Blockchain technology can enable payments and settlements to be performed directly between the sender and the receiver, reducing all fees charged by middlemen and making cros border payments and settlements quickly completed via peer-to-peer. What's more, this technology can not only reduce clearing time, but it also achieves round-the-clock payments and real-time transactions, which makes a cash withdrawal easy and free from hidden costs. According to the calculations of McKinsey, every transaction cost may be reduced to US$15 from about US$26 by merely applying

Blockchain technology to cross border payments and settlements in business-to-business.

SUPPLY CHAIN

Supply chain finance, simply put, is a kind of financing model that provides financial products and services by combining core firms with upstream and downstream enterprises. Funds here serve as a solvent of the supply chain, aiming to increase the liquidity of businesses.

In the current supply chain finance system, the supply chain of a particular commodity includes purchasing raw material, producing an intermediate product and final product, and selling the product to consumers through sales networks. This process puts suppliers, manufacturers, distributors, retailers, and customers together as a whole.[18]

Before

Manual operation entails unpredictable risks.

After

Smart contract of Blockchain can automatically complete financial service so as to reduce risks of manual operations.

Fig. 4-3: Blockchain plus supply chains.

---

18 "Supply Chain Finance" [EB/OL]. [2017-05-18].http://www. tceic.com/169959736i 85ki3g86i2i522.html.

With its open and traceable feature, Blockchain technology can program and digitalize any paper-based process, making it less labor-extensive. In a Blockchain-based system, all involved parties can share files using a decentralized ledger. Smart contracts make it possible for payments to be made when requirements for time and results are met, which not only maximizes efficiency, but also dramatically reduces manual errors. According to the calculation of McKinsey, Blockchain technology has the potential to help worldwide banks save US$100 million to US$1.6 billion brought about by operating risks.

INFORMATION

Once Blockchain technology, with its immutable features, is applied to banking systems, client information and transaction records will become tamper-resistant and immune to any

Doubtful information can be tampered with and deleted.

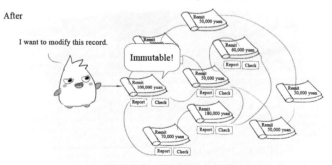

Distributed storage is immutable and trackable.

Fig. 4-4: Blockchain plus information.

human invention as soon as they are confirmed, which helps banks identify abnormal transactions and prevent deception. Besides, banks can develop an information system with shared ledgers based on Blockchain technology to detect and analyze the transactions of users on any nodes. The system can immediately report to the upper layer once abnormal situations occur, thus effectively preventing illegal activities like swindling and money laundering.

Securities

In the securities business, Initial Public Offerings and securities transactions often require the long-term involvement of third parties, leading to attenuated processing and considerable cost for stock issue and transaction. With Blockchain technology, however, investors and institutions are able to complete IPO and free trade on a decentralized trading platform that operates twenty-four hours a day, without the involvement and intervention of third parties.

Fig. 4-5: Blockchain plus security.

For securities traders and practitioners in investment banking, Blockchain helps transform business directions, within which underwriting and resource acquisition will weaken, while the ability to provide professional securities consulting services for investment and finance customers will be strengthened.

INSURANCE

The heart of the traditional insurance business lies in insurance institutions that are responsible for capital pooling, investment, and claim settlement, resulting in substantial operating and management costs. However, Blockchain technology promises to turn the mutual insurance model into a reality. This model enables participants to make payments directly to patients without the intervention of third parties. Therefore, capital pooling and allotment will become transparent and cut operating costs. At the same time, insurance institutions can

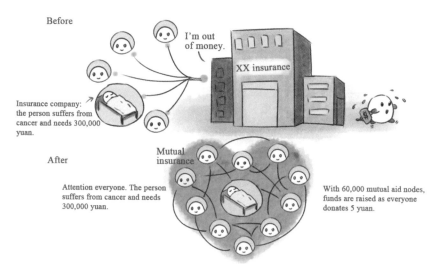

Fig. 4-7: Blockchain plus insurance.

choose to transform themselves into insurance consultancies, which helps them minimize risk.

Case One: OKLink

As Blockchain gains prominence, governments, large financial institutions, and enterprises around the world have begun to invest heavily in the study of this technology. OKLink of OKCoin, the leading global Bitcoin exchange, is a global financial network based on Blockchain technology and also China's first commercialized Blockchain application, which is devoted to promoting global value transmission efficiency. At the same time, OKLink improves the experience of global senders. This application is available in more than twenty countries and regions, including China, Japan, Korea, and Southeast Asian nations. OKCoin's primary clients are mostly small and medium-sized financial participants, including banks, remittance companies, and financial platforms on the Internet. Its transaction value stands at tens of millions of dollars per month.

Previously, we have mentioned the weakness of traditional cross border remittance, like a long cycle and high cost. Based on Blockchain technology, however, OKLink operates under the decentralized system and enables users to made cross border transfers with lower cost and higher speed. In this way, payments and settlements can be completed directly between the sender and the receiver, and all fees normally charged by intermediaries can also be saved. The whole network caps expenses at only 0.5 percent based on the average rate, doesn't charge any hidden fees, and receives money quickly.

Partners of OKLink have access to checking their transactions, as all transactions are traceable. Blockchain technology can make sure that transactions are tamper-resistant and not falsifiable, and its Blockchain-based global financial remittance network promises to achieve real-time settlements, which means payments equal to settlements, making it easy and convenient for small-sized remittances to cross borders.

Case Two: Automated Hedge Fund LendingRobot Series

LendingRobot, a peer-to-peer lending platform based in Seattle, launched the automated hedge fund LendingRobot Series, which proposed various investment preferences based on algorithms, including Short Term Aggressive, Long Term Aggressive, Short Term Conservative, and Long Term Conservative.

Automated management is the main feature of this fund, which is money-related and needs to reassure its customers, thus making Blockchain technology indispensable. This hedge fund will release a ledger every week in which the amount of every transaction will be recorded in detail.

The ledger will be published under a hash code every week and will be authenticated on Ethereum to ensure the immutability of data.

Emmanuel Marot, CEO of LendingRobot, observed, "All investors know 'don't put all your eggs in one basket.' But that is much easier to know than to do in practice, as it is a complicated process for investors to consider investment projects, and investors are expected to be experts in certain fields. Therefore, we launched LendingRobot Series using intelligent control technique and Blockchain technology to enable investors to understand investment values of lending, thus promoting them to invest on our platform more comfortably."

General hedge funds often charge 2 percent management fees and 20 percent performance fees, while LendingRobot only charges a management fee of 1 percent, caps fund expenses at 0.59 percent, and doesn't take a cut for performance.

INTERNET MANAGEMENT

Blockchain technology also is of great advantage to security management on the Internet and the authentication field. It is being used in various place such as social networks, ID cards, and academic credential authentications. In this chapter, I will focus on the Blockchain-based ID card.

What will happen when Blockchain meets ID cards? What will it look like if ID cards exist in the Blockchain world? Let's figure out a miraculous phrase, "distributed smart identification system," that is, the "ID card" in Blockchain.

The ID card is a wonderful thing, and though it is inconspicuous, it seems that we can't do anything and go anywhere without it. It is used to prove a person's identity; we need to

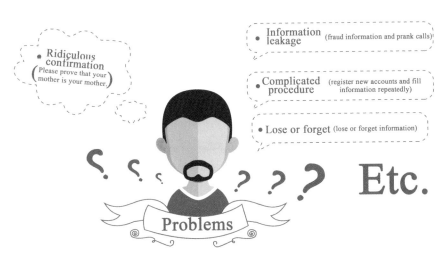

Fig. 4-10: The ID issue.

use it to check in to flights and buy train tickets. Once it is lost or appropriated, or when one forgets to bring it, the owner faces disaster.

If you are still concerned about various issues concerning ID cards, then the smart identification system based on Blockchain technology may dissipate your worries, as your passport photo, online profile, and an irreversible creation data of keys and a key identifier will be present on your Blockchain ID card. At the same time, this ID card also has a signature line, an exclusive QR code, a transaction number, and hash algorithm proof.

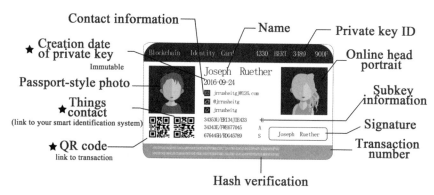

Fig. 4-11: Blockchain-based ID card.

Three steps for creating and using ID cards are detailed below:

First, have a unique name.

Then others can search for your Blockchain-based ID. As long as you carefully keep your password, it will be impossible for others to occupy your name.

Second, create and confirm your personal profile.

Connect your Blockchain-based ID card with your social network profile to prove that the card is yours and confirm your personal information.

Third, start to use your Blockchain-based ID card.

Share your Blockchain-based ID card on your website, social network profile, and business cards so that others can easily search for you on the Internet.

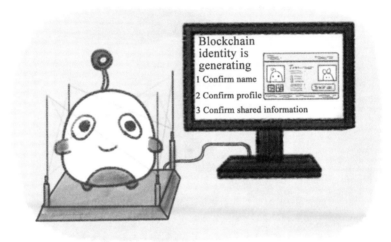

Fig. 4-12: Creating a Blockchain-based ID.

A Blockchain-based ID boasts the following advantages: first, it can safely and conveniently crack the problem of information loss. Second, it is tamper-resistant and will not be lost forever.

If everyone has a Blockchain-based ID card, it means that one has a complete, unique, and permanent entry that records all one's lifetime transactions. In the future, it may take quite some time for Blockchain-based ID cards to connect all personal information together, but it promises to immediately replace ID cards, fingerprints, passports, and other identification tools.

Of course, if one day you do acquire a Blockchain-based ID card, please store the key carefully, as any operations require

Fig. 4-13: Advantages of a Blockchain-based ID card.

you to use the key to open your personal account. Meanwhile, please back up this unique key because only you have access to it.

Once Blockchain-based ID cards are issued, iris recognition and other biometric recognition technologies may be out of date. After all, if a hacker wants to attack a system, he needs to first intrude into it before tampering. However, in a Blockchain system, login is regarded as a kind of "transaction behavior."

If one wants to log into a system that has applied Blockchain technology through assuming the identity of others,

Fig. 4-14: Blockchain IDs that can record your whole life.

it means that he needs to log into data chains on hundreds of millions of computers, which is almost impossible. If that day comes, technologies like fingerprint or iris scanning will become unnecessary.

Case One: Holberton School of Software Engineering

On October 2015, Holberton School of Software Engineering, based in San Francisco, announced that they would use Blockchain to record students' academic performance, becoming the world's first school to authenticate its academic certificates via Blockchain technology.

Sylvain Kalache, cofounder of the school, said that his school understands it is difficult for companies to verify academic certificates when recruiting, so they adopted Blockchain technology to authenticate students' academic certificates.

Kalache said, "For employers, it avoids having them spend valuable time checking candidates' educational credentials by having to call universities or to pay a third party to do the job." At the same time, using Blockchain helps save the school money by not having to build and operate its own database of records. He also said, "Our students are very happy about the fact that their academic qualifications will be authenticated in Blockchain. They also see the potential of this technology as many companies have been massively investing in the Block-chain, and they are proud to be part of the school that was the first to use it."[19]

Case Two: SecureKey, an Identity Authentication Company in Canada

SecureKey, an authentication and verification service com-pany based in Canada, and the Digital ID and Authentication Council of Canada have received funds from the affiliated research center of the Department of Homeland Security, and the two will work together to build a Blockchain-based dig-ital identity network. Now SecureKey is developing a confi-dential program, which is known as "triple blind." Once this program is installed, for example, when a consumer inputs his account and password to log into a banking system, the bank cannot see where the data are going, and the recipient cannot see which bank is used or any bank account information. As a middleman, SecureKey is similarly "blind" and cannot see who is using the services. That is what "triple blind" means.

19 "Holberton School Begins Tracking Student Academic Credentials on the BitcoinBlockchain" [EB/OL]. (2016–05–18) [2017–05–18].https://Bitcoinmagazine .com/articles/holberton-school-begins-tracking-student-academic-credentials -on-theBitcoin-Blockchain-1463605176/.

Andre Boysen, chief identity officer of SecureKey, said in an interview, "In today's world, every organization acts on its own. Digital identity is bigger than any one organization . . . it takes a village to make digital identity work."[20]

In an era that witnesses technology developing by leaps and bounds, humans must find trustworthy technology when verifying personal identity to avoid identity theft. SecureKey and the DIACC are currently working on this technology.

ENERGY

Whenever it comes to a business model in the energy sector, the word *Blockchain* will be mentioned. As this technology gains prominence, its application in the energy sector is full of fantasy, leading the trend of "Internet Plus" intelligent energy resources. In this chapter, we are going to share some views from *Prospect on Blockchain's Application in Energy Internet* and at the same time briefly explain them. In general, Blockchain is mainly applied to three aspects of the energy sector: electric power, ecosystem, and the intelligent regulation of energy.

Electric Power

One of the important features of Blockchain is that data are immutable, which is closely related to this technology's application in the electric power industry. With Blockchain technology, the "Past and Present" per unit of electricity will be recorded in the Blockchain network. For example, a unit of electricity generated in a nuclear power plant on a particular

---

20 "Canada's SecureKey to Build a Blockchain Digital Identity Network with US Grant" [EB/OL]. (2017–02–15) [2017–05–18].https://www.cryptocoinsnews.com /canadas-securekey-to-build-Blockchain-digital-identity-network-with-us-grant/.

day is transmitted into my home through a wire and is consumed as I keep the lights on for several hours.

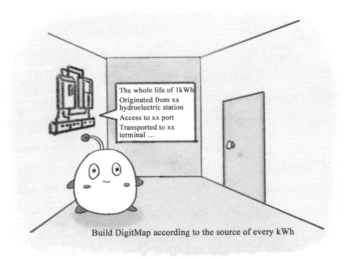

Fig. 4-15: Blockchain plus electric power.

In the future, Blockchain plus electric power may have the following development directions:

1. Every unit of electricity can be traceable in order to avoid power theft and electric leakage at the root. With all behaviors recorded in an immutable ledger, situations that appear out of nowhere only to disappear suddenly will be dealt with as an abnormal circumstance.
2. You will be able to sell surplus electricity to your neighbors. Our current electric system has had something to do with intelligence, since electricity purchase and blackout are completed through an intelligent electricity meter. However, the decentralized Blockchain

technology can even enable you to sell your surplus electricity to your neighbors. In the future, we can build a map concerning each unit of electricity. For example, suppose that the solar generator at your home can generate one unit of electricity, but you only use half of it every day. The surplus electricity will then be stored in the network. Therefore, your neighbors can directly buy electricity from you when they need power. In this way, Blockchain makes it possible to share distributed energy resources.

Ecosystem

The combination of Blockchain, IoT, and big data has the potential to build a "Utopian" energy ecosystem. Just as a simple example, suppose that one day an energy ecosystem is formed with the characteristics of these three technologies, and then the equipment suppliers, professional operation providers, owners who use the equipment, and financial systems

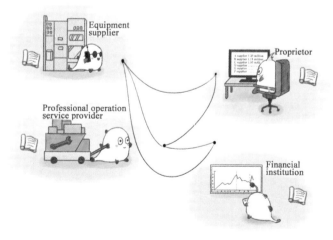

Fig. 4-16: Interactive and reliable ecosystems.

responsible for money circulation and price quotation need to take tests in this system. Every party in this system will be informed of a password inquiry, with which he or she can check any action taken by anybody in this system. In this way, all involved parties can form a relationship featuring interactive supervision and trust. The system can offer an optimal plan for the owner through calculation according to big data analysis and autonomously makes a purchase or conducts maintenance via financial institutions through smart contracts.

Intelligent Regulation of Energy
In the future, with Blockchain technology, intelligent regulation of energy can be achieved as smart devices can be connected to Internet information. Imagine that when webcams in an urban area capture the sudden blackout of a transmission facility and match it with information provided by other related notes—like a siren or lights in a specific area suddenly powering off—and then confirm the situation. The above

Fig. 4-17: Smart control of energy.

information will be transmitted to the maintenance department, which will then send related maintenance equipment based on smart contracts to carry out repairs on the spot. In this way, the age of intelligence regulation will bring more convenience and comfort to our daily lives.

Case One: TransActive Grid, Energy Transmission Project
LO3 Energy, a Blockchain startup in New York, has worked with the technology giant Siemens to develop TransActive Grid, an energy transmission project based on Ethereum, in which customers can resell their unused electricity to those who need it. LO3 Energy has received a patent for the decentralized energy transmission awarded by the U.S. Patent and Trademark Office.

Ralf Christian, CEO of the Energy Management Division at Siemens, said, "We're convinced that our microgrid control and automation solutions, in combination with the Blockchain technology of our partner LO3 Energy, will provide additional value for our customers on the utilities side."

Both companies said that they would test the microgrids powered by Blockchain technology in New York and other parts of the world, hoping to spread these Blockchain-based microgrids all over the world.

Case Two: Energy Bitcoin Lab
On May 15, 2016, the world's first energy Blockchain laboratory was officially launched, which was founded by four people. This lab mainly focuses on developing Blockchain platforms, from which the collaboration tools will be used for the development, auditing, registration, and transaction

of financial products. Cao Yin, the founding partner and the Principle Analyst of China Cinda Securities, said when interviewed by TMTPost, "In the future, energy storage is more likely to be developed on the basis of sharing economy. The utilization ratio of stored energy bought by a single company is very low as it is impossible for those energy resources to be fully utilized within 24 hours a day." However, with Blockchain technology, energy storage will share the same features as the taxis of Didi and Uber. Neighbors can utilize their energy storage facilities through the sharing of use rights and will receive payment based on earnings made through energy storage.[21]

Fig. 4-18: Target of Energy Blockchain laboratory.

GOVERNMENT

With decentralized, immutable, trustworthy, and traceable features, Blockchain plus the government also has the potential to transform society.

---

21 "The world's first energy Blockchain laboratory was launched" [EB/OL]. (2016-05-18) [2017-05-18]. http://news.bjx.com.cn/html/20160518/734100. shtml.

Basic Information Protection

How does the government information system protect our data? Information from subordinate departments will be gathered for governmental authorities, and the latter will have the right to use them. In this model, a hacker only needs to hack a centralized router when attacking governmental information systems. Once he succeeds, information stored in this router is likely to be leaked, damaged, lost, and criminally compromised.

However, the application of Blockchain technology is expected to increase the security of information systems significantly. In this way, government information will be distributed and stored in each node, and every department will own a general ledger, which is hash-encrypted, immutable, and resistant to leak. Under such circumstances, if a hacker successfully attacks a single node, neither will government

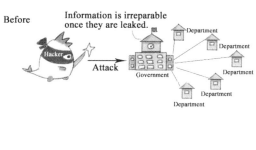

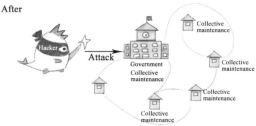

Fig. 4-19: Blockchain plus basic information protection.

information be stolen nor the system influenced, as other nodes also store the same entire ledger. Moreover, it is useless to modify the data in a node, as this action cannot be recognized by the whole network.

Identification of Citizens

Do you want to prove that you have gotten married? Please go to the Civil Affairs Bureau for a marriage certificate. Do you want to prove that your mother is yours? Sorry, no such government department can issue this kind of document. But yet another department claims that I cannot fulfill certain formalities without this certificate. Well . . . please go to other related departments to consult.

Citizen identification is regarded as an indispensable part of government affairs, but it's also time-consuming and labor-intensive. Blockchain technology, however, enables all one's information to be stored in one's "address," and it can be used

Fig. 4-20: Blockchain plus identity authentication.

whenever needed. The immutable feature of this technology also dissipates people's worries about whether their certificates are valid or not. The Blockchain-based citizen identification system can not only effectively cut the waste of social resources, but also ensure the highest level of authenticity, and therefore receive the recognition of all people.

Government Affairs Information Transparency

Currently, government information around the world is hardly transparent, as we only know established laws but have no idea about how they are enacted. Therefore, it is often a scapegoat who will stand out and be responsible for the errors of laws, resulting in a chaotic situation lacking in supervision.

Fig. 4-21: Blockchain plus transparency of government affairs.

Blockchain technology has the potential to increase the transparency of government affairs and enables policy implementation to be free from the disturbance of external factors.

At the same time, the traceable feature of policies also helps us make more prudent decisions.

Government Supervision on Taxation

Fig. 4-22: Blockchain plus government taxation supervision.

Tax evasion and tax fraud are serious issues around the world. Some companies and individuals evade taxes by cooking the books. However, with Blockchain technology, a company can build a distributed ledger when it is established, which is a database recording every transaction during all operations. It also can perform mutual authentication with the distributed ledgers of other companies through smart contracts.

As every account is immutable and traceable, tax evasion and tax fraud can be effectively eliminated. What's more, once these illegal conducts are revealed, they will be recorded on Blockchain and become a permanent record.

Public Bidding for Projects

In the bidding for government projects, there has been a phenomenon known as "those who have good relationships with governments win." When the requirement for a budget is met, who will win the bid for the project, to some extent, depends on the bidder's relationship with the government. Many companies have to sit and wait after bidding, and in most cases, they have no idea about why they fail to win the bidding. Sometimes, even though they didn't win the project, their bidding plans may be used in the follow-up constructions. What companies can do is to comfort themselves that what happens is just a coincidence. With Blockchain technology, however, all bidding information can be transparent, and only specific people have access to related records, which, to some degree, can curb corruption. Imagine that when corruption records are stored in a ledger to which your boss always has access, maybe corruption will no longer be so blatant and ubiquitous.

Fig. 4-23: Blockchain plus public bidding for projects.

Supervision on Bailout Funds

Many people are willing to take part in charitable activities, but it becomes increasingly difficult for us to trust those charities when explosive scandals like corruption, embezzlement, and publicity stunts are undermining their legitimacy. What's more, sometimes our inappropriate donations may become a burden for society. For example, we may send our used clothes to a relief service station whose address we found by searching on the Internet, but this station may be overloaded with old clothes that are unavailable to another station.

Fig. 4-24: Blockchain plus supervision on bailout funds.

Now, Blockchain technology enables us to monitor how individual donations are used. For instance, suppose that you donated one yuan to a charity on Children's Day last year, and records on Blockchain showed that the money had turned into grapes in a fruit bowl for left-behind children in a center. Transparent and traceable charities will not waste our money and kindness.

Issue Lottery Tickets Online

Online lottery sales are suspended after a brief prevalence, and sellers who cheat consumers are the culprits. The cheating process operates like this: when a person buys a lottery ticket, instead of buying a real one in the lottery center, the seller turns his store into a small gambling center. If a person wins 100 yuan, the seller will directly transfer this amount of money into his or her account; if you fail to win a prize, the two yuan you spent on a lottery ticket will be earned by the seller. It is in this way that those ponies make money. However, when you win 200 million yuan, which is not affordable for the seller, the latter can do nothing but escape.

Fig. 4-25: Blockchain plus issuing online lottery tickets.

Blockchain technology, in combination with smart contracts, can prevent online lottery centers from cheating consumers. Every transaction will become transparent and traceable, and the buyer will receive the money from smart contracts after he or she wins the prize.

Case One: "E-Residents" of Estonia

The Estonian government plans to issue digital IDs to people around the world, therefore encouraging online trading within Estonia. Although foreigners who get a "digital citizenship" are not given residency, they can trade with Estonians on the Internet. E-Residents can set digital signatures, as well as verify and encrypt certificates, contracts, and other files. Once bank accounts are opened, e-Residents in Estonia can make transfers by controlling the accounts through electronic banks to any country around the world.[22]

Case Two: Voting System—Follow My Vote

Follow My Vote is devoted to developing a secure and efficient end-to-end voting system that is also openly sourced and auditable through the adaptation of Blockchain technology, thus avoiding security holes during the vote.

Instead of queuing and waiting in front of a polling booth, voters can cast votes at home using a webcam and government-issued ID. The virtual electorate could then theoretically watch the election in real-time because of Blockchain auditing features; the distributed ledger on Blockchain also makes sure that votes are anonymous and immutable. Additionally, each

---

22 "Estonian Government Partners with Bitnation to Offer Blockchain Notarization Services to e-Residents" [EB/OL]. (2015-11-30) [2017-05-18]. https://Bitcoinmagazine .com/articles/estonian-government-partners-with-bitnation-to-offerBlock- chain-notarization-services-to-e-residents-1448915243/.

voter can change his or her vote at any time during the election using a private key and unique voter ID.

Nathan Hourt is the cofounder and CTO of Follow My Vote. He considers paper-based voting systems to be impractical. Apart from the obvious issue of scale, they are precariously reliant on the procedural security of officials conducting their jobs correctly and honestly, Hourt argues.[23]

HEALTH CARE

Blockchain has made the demography database and health data transactions obsolete. Blockchain technology can improve data security and save explicit and hidden costs. If new medical records become a reality, the tragedy of poor-quality child vaccinations that occurred in early 2016 will never happen again.

In its "2016–2020 Blockchain Technology In-Depth Survey and Investment Prospects Report," China Investment Advisors divide the application of Blockchain technology in the medical field into the following areas: digital clinical record, "DNA Wallet," medical anticounterfeiting, and protein folding.[24]

Digital Clinical Record

Traditionally in China, the clinical records in different hospitals stay isolated. If the patient refuses or forgets to provide his or her clinical records to the doctor, the hospital has no other

---

23 "Block The Vote: Could Blockchain Technology Cybersecure Elections?" [EB/OL]. (2016–08–30) [2017–05–18].https://www.forbes.com/sites/realspin/2016/08/30/block-the-vote-could-Blockchain-technology-cybersecure-elections/#1097f71b2ab.

24 "Analysis of Blockchain's application in medical field" [EB/OL]. [2017–05–18]. https://wenku. baidu.com/view/d551f47a6529647d2628524f.html.

access to it, which hinders the diagnosis and treatment process. Instead, Blockchain technology can be applied to create digital records for everyone to store their clinical history and medical data.

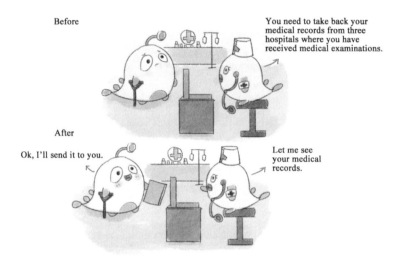

Fig. 4-26: Blockchain plus clinical records.

DNA wallet

DNA wallet is a Blockchain-based system where users can store their genetic and clinical data and access those data with their

Fig. 4-27: Blockchain plus the DNA wallet.

private key. This will facilitate pharmaceutical developments because enterprises, research institutions, and other organizations can apply for authorization to use these data for medical research.

Medicine Anticounterfeiting
Blockchain technology can be used to prevent medicine counterfeiting. The theoretical foundation is similar to identity verification, leveraging the traceability of Blockchain to label crude drugs and pharmaceutical products. Thus the fraudulent medications produced by counterfeiters will find no market, since consumers can check the numeration of the drug to verify whether it is genuine or not.

Fig. 4-28: Blockchain plus drug anticounterfeiting.

Protein Folding
The process of protein folding is very difficult to model. Stanford University has previously relied on a very expensive supercomputer to simulate the process of protein folding. However,

the disadvantages of this approach are obvious: enormous cost and a possible single point of failure. Using Blockchain technology can create a distributed network to assist in folding proteins. Each node in the network can call on the computing power of the entire network when performing operations. When 10,000 computers work together to calculate data for you, there is no need to purchase an expensive supercomputer.

Fig. 4-29: Blockchain plus protein folding.

Case One: Guardtime and the Estonian eHealth Foundation

Data security startup Guardtime has announced a partnership with the Estonian eHealth Foundation that will see it deploy a Blockchain-based system to secure over 1 million patient healthcare records.

Under the deal, the foundation will integrate Guardtime's keyless signature infrastructure (KSI) Blockchain into the foundation's Oracle database engine to provide "real-time visibility" into the state of patient records.

A spokesperson for the company said:

"In guarding sensitive records, the danger is that they could be altered, deleted, improperly changed or updated, affected by hackers, malware, system issues, etc. The Blockchain in this case can prove the integrity of the record, and everything that has happened to it over time."

Margus Auväärt, who heads the eHealth Foundation, said that Guardtime would allow it to maintain real-time awareness of health records.

"It enables us to react to any incidents immediately, before potentially larger-scale damages can occur," Auväärt said.[25]

Case Two: Brontech Health Care Service Platform
Australia's Sydney–based startup, Brontech, is utilizing Blockchain to create a platform that establishes trust and security within the healthcare system. Brontech describes decentralization:

In the previous two decades the internet has reshaped our lives like nothing else before, however, today most of our online interactions require some kind of impartial third-party mediator. Lately, these mediators tend to build business models that are gravitating around using and/or misusing the data collected during the process of mediation. Moreover, the activities that are needed to establish the trust among the stakeholder of a certain process are placing huge overhead in terms of time and money. The

---

25 "Blockchain Startup to Secure 1 Million e-Health Records in Estonia" [EB/OL]. (2016–03–03) [2017–05–18].http://www.coindesk.com/Blockchain-startupaims -to-secure-1-million-estonian-health-records/.

Blockchain offers a way to resolve these issues that sur-round the traditional transaction systems by making trust obsolete and in the same time making these interactions safer, cheaper and faster.

The cofounder of Brontech, Emma Poposka, explained how they are trying to achieve this with their platform and identity module Cyph MD: "We are trying to build a digital identity that's like bulletproof, and that can be used by everybody, even by people who don't necessarily have legal identities in their countries."[26]

COPYRIGHT

Copyright is now a hot topic, while Blockchain attains even more attention. Ordinary people have already known the con-cept of copyright through series of movies adapted from pop-ular novels being released one after one, such as *Tiny Times*, *So Young*, and *Time Raiders*. We all know that copyright is equal to money. In other words, he who holds more copyrights in hand will have the more discursive power.

High profits incite many battles over copyrights. Examples are plentiful. The media exposed that *Goodbye Mr. Loser* com-pletely plagiarized an old American movie. Both the author and scriptwriter of *The Legend of Miyue* insisted on their owner-ship of the copyright. This phenomenon is especially common

---

26 "Australian Startup Cyph MD Uses Blockchain Technology for Data Sharing in Healthcare" [EB/OL]. (2016–08–09) [2017–05–18].http://www.the-Blockchain .com/2016/08/09/australian-startup-cyph-md-uses-Blockchain-technolog y-datasharing-healthcare/.

in *The Grave Robbers' Chronicles*, which has inspired so many derivative works.

Fig. 4-30: Blockchain plus copyright protection.

The causes of these questions are the ownership and protection of copyright. It's a burning issue but difficult to solve due to the high cost of safeguarding original writers' rights and interests. They are often too mentally and physically exhausted to protect their rights. But now, Blockchain could provide support to writers and allow them to defend themselves instantly.

Let's see how to solve copyright issues through the use of Blockchain technology.

First, claim your ownership and timestamp it.

Creators can upload their original works and the respective agreements to Blockchain. Then a corresponding hash of these files will be generated. The cryptographic hash of these files can be inserted into a transaction afterward. When that transaction is mined into a block, the timestamp of the block becomes part of these files. This digital certificate, composed of a hash and a timestamp, will solve issues of "proof of existence" and the chronology of the creation of works to some degree.

Second, trace the ownership and the whole process.

Blockchain could trace throughout all sections relating to copyright use and transaction and achieve tracing of the whole process, which is irreversible and tamper-resistant. Besides, the application of Blockchain technology could also solve issues of intangible asset verification and value assessment to some degree.

Fig. 4-31: The difficulty in protecting copyrights.

China's social publishing platform "appreciates" the copyright and even proposes the idea that "the copyright of a work should be verified in the process of its creation." In other words, record the whole process, from an initial creative spark to a created work, thus enabling it to enter into transactions with verified rights from the beginning.

"Appreciation" function expects to standardize the exercise and tracing of work rights through smart contracts. At the same time, it introduces copyright services to transactions when a project is still under creation.

This could be regarded as a package copyright service in the Blockchain by which copyright would be verified without any modification, from an initial idea to a final product. Let's imagine that if Blockchain copyright certificates could be expanded on a large scale, those copycats would not be as furious as they are now.

It seems prudent to use Blockchain technology to solve issues of copyright protection. However, it actually faces three major challenges:

1. The commercialization and popularization of Blockchain technology are still in the development stage. Though the concept of Blockchain is known to most people, its penetration rate is still low, just as VR.

2. More efforts are needed to propose, enact, and revise laws related to Blockchain technology. Popularizing the concept of Blockchain is difficult. As a result, there is no major copyright issue that has been successfully solved by the use of Blockchain technology. Without a legal basis, Blockchain certificates are still just a concept.

3. There is an enormous cost in generating a hash. A hash is generated based on file size, creation time, type, creator, and so on, so slight variation of any information would invoke great changes. No one could predict the next hash, and there is no software

Fig. 4-32: Three challenges in Blockchain's
application in copyright protection.

to modify it. Therefore, with process costs increasing, if no giant is willing to take the lead in developing such software, there is no answer to when Blockchain could be used to protect copyrights.

Case One: Babyghost & BitSE

At Shanghai's Fashion Week 2016, trendy fashion label Babyghost teamed up with Shanghai-based Blockchain-as-a-Service (BaaS) company, and BitSE presented twenty new products. Those in attendance at the event had a unique opportunity, as each piece was embedded with a VeChain chip. By simply scanning each piece of clothing, they received an interactive memory revealing information about their piece and its journey. Later on, should customers want to sell it secondhand, information about their purchase and wearing of the item would be recorded on the chip, and this interactive memory would be provided to the next buyer, according to BitSE.[27]

Case Two: Blockchain and Music

Imogen Heap released her new single *Tiny Human* via the Ethereum Blockchain in October 2015. Users could get the permission to use this MP3 file just after putting ETH into their accounts. This transaction allowed Heap and her group to obtain income directly and promptly while at the same time users gained access.[28]

IoT

If we compare the development of the Internet to the speed of an express train, then the combination of Blockchain and IoT is like taking a rocket. The interconnection of all things will be an irresistible trend in the future. For example, with a smart home system, we can simply use our smartphones to control all electric appliances from a distance. Recent years have

27 "Babyghost and VeChain: Fashion on the Blockchain" [EB/OL]. (2016-10-18) [2017-05-18].https://Bitcoinmagazine.com/articles/babyghost-and-vechain-fashionon-the-Blockchain-1476807653/.

28 "Blockchain Going for a Song: New Tech Tunes Up Music Industry" [EB/OL]. (2016-05-22) [2017-05-18].https://cointelegraph.com/news/Blockchain-going-for-asong-new-tech-tunes-up-music-industry.

witnessed the stride of technology, including the rapid evolution of IoT. According to the latest statistical report released by International Data Corporation, by 2020, the global Internet of Things market will grow to 3 trillion US dollars, while the global IoT device will reach 30 billion.

Fig. 4-33: Simplified IoT.

Blockchain technology can create a reliable connection among the applications on the IoT without high costs, and its decentralization consensus can help to strengthen the security and privacy of the system. Besides, the combination of Blockchain technology and smart contracts can turn each smart device into a network node that can be self-maintained and self-adjusted. These nodes can exchange information, verify identities, and conduct transactions with strangers on a predefined basis.

Take cable network as an example. Existing cable networks have widespread security risks and waste phenomena. Imagine how safe, convenient, and affordable the intelligent cable trays will be. Once a smart cable tray encounters a lightning strike, it can generate an accident report immediately and notify the maintenance team what to bring and where to go for repair. At the same time, intelligent cable trays can also temporarily assign signal transmission tasks to nearby cable poles, because they belong to the same network. As a result, telecommunications companies do not have to spend extensively on on-site repairing, and communications will resume as soon as possible.

In the world of Blockchain plus IoT, each cable tray is identifiable and cannot participate in operations without identity. The Blockchain used for identity authentication is the core of the smart cable network. Engineers will set up a unique line for each device (cable bridge) and then store this line along with the identity in a distributed ledger.

Distributed ledgers can guarantee that these devices only continue to operate after they receive the fee. In the event of

Fig. 4-34: Blockchain plus IoT.

damage, the smart cable network reacts quickly and automatically finds new lines to prevent large areas of communication from being interrupted.

These are just some of the ideas about the intelligent cable tray. If you expand your imagination, you will find items ranging from the smallest sensor to enormous mechanical devices, are all things that can be connected to the vast IoT.

The IoT has a wide range of applications, covering smart transportation, environmental protection, government work, public safety, smart cities, smart homes, environmental monitoring, industrial monitoring, and food traceability. The greatest challenge facing the development of the IoT is not merely to establish a decentralized Internet of Things, but to establish a universal IoT that can continuously expand while ensuring privacy and security so that current participants can conduct transactions without losing trust. However, not all participants in the IoT are trustworthy. After all, there can be hundreds of billions of them, some of whom can even be

Fig. 4-35: Blockchain connected to everything.

corrupt. Therefore, it is imperative to build a verification and consensus mechanism.

It is foreseeable that in the future, billions of people, and hundreds of billions of machines on the planet, will all be connected to a Blockchain network, and people will interact with machines, and machines will interact with machines to conduct efficient communication, trade, and payment. Humankind is accelerating their steps toward an era where goods and services are almost free, and the world of Blockchain plus IoT, a world of decentralization and collaborative sharing, will be the destination.[29]

Case One: Filament
Filament has raised $5m in Series A funding led by Bullpen Capital, including contributions from Verizon Ventures and Samsung Ventures.

This decision by Samsung Ventures, the capital arm of the consumer electronics giant Samsung, marks its first public investment in a Blockchain industry firm and notably follows its participation in IBM's Blockchain proof of concept ADEPT.

Announced in January, ADEPT used the Bitcoin and Ethereum networks to enable communication between devices as part of a wider transition toward connected consumer devices known as the Internet of Things (IoT).

Cofounder and CEO Eric Jennings framed Filament as a decentralized IoT software stack that uses the Bitcoin Blockchain to enable devices to hold unique identities on a public

29 "Filament Nets $5 Million for Blockchain-Based Internet of Things Hardware" [EB/OL]. (2015–08–18) [2017–05–18].http://www.coindesk.com /filamentnets-5-million-for-Blockchain-based-internet-of-things-hardware/.

ledger. By creating a smart device directory, he said, Filament's IoT devices will be able to communicate, execute smart contracts, and send microtransactions securely.

Given this vision, Jennings sees his project as similar in ethos to ADEPT, even though it will target the industrial market, enabling large firms in industries such as oil, gas, manufacturing, and agriculture to unlock new efficiencies.

Jennings told CoinDesk:

"Almost all these companies have the same concern—'What is my IoT strategy?' Many of these companies are good at what they build but they don't have a lot of expertise in mesh networking or Blockchains, but they know they need to connect these networks to gain efficiencies or risk going out of business."

Case Two: IBM & Samsung

IBM has unveiled its proof of concept for ADEPT, a system developed in partnership with Samsung that uses elements of Bitcoin's underlying design to build a distributed network of devices—a decentralized Internet of Things.

The ADEPT concept, or Autonomous Decentralized Peer-to-Peer Telemetry, taps Blockchains to provide the backbone of the system, utilizing a mix of proof-of-work and proof-of-stake to secure transactions.

IBM and Samsung chose three protocols—BitTorrent (file sharing), Ethereum (smart contracts), and TeleHash (peer-to-peer messaging)—to underpin the ADEPT concept. ADEPT was formally unveiled at CES 2015 in Las Vegas.

According to the draft paper, Blockchains deployed within the ADEPT system would serve as a ledger of existence for billions of devices that would autonomously broadcast transactions between peers in a three-tier system of peer devices and architecture. By using an implementation of the Bitcoin protocol, ADEPT could serve as a bridge between many devices at low cost.

The paper adds:

"Applying the Blockchain concept to the world of [Internet of Things] offers fascinating possibilities. Right from the time a product completes final assembly, it can be registered by the manufacturer into a universal Blockchain representing its beginning of life. Once sold, a dealer or end customer can register it to a regional Blockchain (a community, city or state)."[30]

The draft paper outlines several of use cases, including several based in domestic settings. When CoinDesk spoke with chief architect Paul Brody in October, he noted that IBM was looking at how, in theory, implementations of the Bitcoin protocol could change the way people live, in both big and small ways.

AGRICULTURE

Relationships among people create mutual trust, and then contacts and exchanges bring forward joint operation. Finally, all humans can enjoy joint development. Blockchain operations perfectly explain that process. As the foundation technology of Bitcoin, Blockchain makes accounting accessible to everyone involved in the network. In other words, all maintain their own identical copy of the ledger, but no one can delete or

---

30 "IBM Reveals Proof of Concept for Blockchain-Powered Internet of Things" [EB/OL]. (2015-01-17) [2017-05-18].http://www.coindesk.com/ibm-revealsproof -concept-Blockchain-powered-internet-things/.

modify it, regardless of institution or individuals. Since Blockchain is highly transparent with great practical utility, could Blockchain and agriculture benefit each other by associating together in China, a vast agricultural country?

Current Situation of China's Agriculture

1. Regarding agricultural production and management, relatively traditional and extensive processes are still used. Additionally, there are no fundamental changes adopted in weather-dependent situations.

2. Concerning the sustainable development of resources, agriculture production in China has consumed lots of resources and energy and seriously destroyed the ecological environment, directly influencing environmental security and people's health.

3. Information exchange and modernization in China's agricultural society is still in the starting stage. The people involved need to introduce more advanced technology to improve the level of intelligent agriculture.

4. In terms of food safety, problems in China continue to emerge due to inadequate legal restraint and supervision, as well as the blind pursuit of maximum profit by some enterprises and individuals. Therefore, people lack sufficient trust in the food safety system. [31]

---

31 "Blockchain plus agriculture' has be realized" [EB/OL]. (2016–10–28) [2017–05–18].http://www.hooshong.com/news/133309.html.

Fig. 4-36: Problems facing China's agriculture today.

Based on the current situation, China's agriculture could combine with Blockchain technology in two ways—commercialization and agricultural insurance.

1. **Commercialization and Blockchain:** Fully transparent in the process of consumption.

   Producers can record all information about their products in Blockchain by the use of Internet identity technology and form a complete trajectory of each of their products in Blockchain.

   For example, if Mr. Wang produces 5kg of non-GM wheat, he would add an initial record into Blockchain about this production. Then, Mr. Wang sells this 5kg of wheat to Mr. Liu in the market, so a new record would be added in Blockchain about the purchase. Later, Mr. Liu sells the wheat to the bakery in the town, and records in Blockchain would be updated to note that the bakery bought 5kg of wheat from Mr. Liu. Then, the bakery makes the wheat into bread. Finally, when consumers purchase the bread, they can find all the production process records after searching the relative information and making an identification.

Before

The package is printed "non-GMO food," but how can I believe it?

I can't bring you to places where wheat grows.

non-GMO food

After

The package is printed "non-GMO food," but how can I believe it?

You can trace the source of this food through the Blockchain network.

non-GMO food

Fig. 4-37: A transparent consuming process.

2. **Agricultural insurance and Blockchain:** Promoting intelligent agriculture.

The combination of Blockchain technology and agricultural insurance could not only effectively reduce insurance fraud, but also simplify handling procedures and upgrade intelligence in insurance compensation. For example, Blockchain will automatically start the process of compensation once it detects an agricultural disaster. In this way, compensation work would become more efficient, and issues of insurance fraud would be readily solved.

Fig. 4-38: The upgrade of smart agriculture.

Case One: The Global Supply Chain of Walmart

Walmart has developed a Blockchain pilot focused on China's massive pork industry supply chain. Built in collaboration with IBM and Beijing's Tsinghua University, the pilot is part of two separate but parallel pushes by Walmart and the Chinese government to make the supply chain data more accurate, and therefore safer. With an estimated $1 trillion to be saved by moving the global supply chain to Blockchain, Walmart stands to not only help China makes its food safer, but will cut corners on cost. IBM's head of global supply chain solutions explained that "the pilot, if implemented, could also give Walmart a bigger slice of China's lucrative pork industry."

In the beginning, the pilot will run on three nodes, one managed by IBM, one by Walmart, and another by an unnamed supplier that wanted to remain anonymous. The head said that by the time the project scales to ten nodes, the industry could save "billions of dollars." That's because when food is sold to a consumer at a Walmart store, each item will have been authenticated using the Blockchain system to create a transparent and secure record. According to a statement, a record created in the distributed ledger can also help the retailer better manage the shelf life of its products in individual stores.[32]

Case Two: The Smart Farms of Filament

According to AgFunderNews, many potential distributed ledger agricultural solutions are emerging. This includes startups like Filament creating concepts like smart farms. With Filament's platform, users connect physical objects and existing networks into "wider networks and applications," turning smart farm technology into a reliable infrastructure. Smart farms are a form of sustainable agriculture that aims to enhance our environmental quality, integrate technology with natural biological cycle controls, and create economic viability within farm operations. Smart farming using Blockchain technology can broadcast tamper-resistant weather data, SMS alerts, machinery protocol, and GPS positioning and can tether many more precise agriculture-related platforms.

Insiders explain the potential for Blockchain growth in the agricultural economy, stating: "Consumer demand for 'clean' food, including organic, is skyrocketing, but producers and manufacturers are often struggling to verify the accuracy of data from farm to table. Blockchain can help. Practical applications of Blockchain technology in the agriculture sector also include minimizing unfair pricing, revealing product origins,

---

32 "Walmart joins hands with IBM and Tsinghua University to start Blockchain pilot program" [EB/OL].(2016–10–20) [2017–05–18]. http://www.sohu.com /a/116621490_448077.

and reducing multinational agricultural influence in favor of more localized economies. In the future, these platforms could also help with remittance to rural regions, as well as other rural farming finance solutions.

"Blockchain technology is continuing to show it can transform many markets and economies in society, and agriculture will be one of them."[33]

CHARITY

Charitable donations are increasing in popularity while this industry still has problems that have persisted for years. In some cases, it prevents people from donating at all.

The Charities Aid Foundation recently released a twenty-page report, "Giving Unchained—Philanthropy and the Blockchain," which examines how Blockchain technology will affect the way charities raise money and operate. The report claims that Blockchain technology could change the way people contribute to charities and the way funds address social problems.

According to the twenty-page report, charities in the US brought in over $2 trillion in revenue last year, $373 billion of which came from charitable contributions. This report also analyses the benefits of Blockchain technology in philanthropy:

1. Reduced transaction costs
Transactions on Blockchain do not require a middleman (banks or other institutes) but are directly donated to specified individuals or institutes, which will effectively reduce transaction costs.

---

33 "Blockchain Will Transform the Agriculture Industry" [EB/OL]. (2016–09–06) [2017–05–18].https://news.Bitcoin.com/Blockchain-agriculture-industry/.

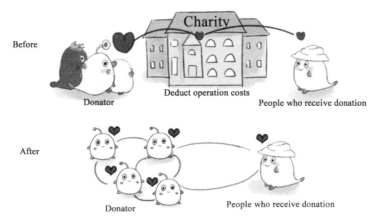

Fig. 4-39: Reducing transaction costs.

2. Increased Transparency

Blockchain technology can make the donation process more transparent. Each donation will be directly recorded in a distributed ledger database, and the transparent records are open to access and tamper-proof. An individual donor would literally be able to track their donation right through a ledger.

3. Enhanced Trust

Fig. 4-40: Increasing transparency.

Blockchain technology offers real opportunities to build trust. The removal of the need for third parties means that the new 2.0 charities and nonprofits would no longer have to rely on other institutions such as banks, lawyers, and government bodies in the same way.

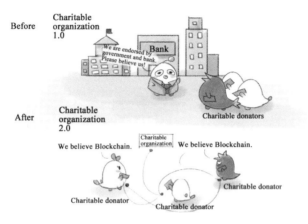

Fig. 4-41: Strengthening trust.

Case: The BitGive Foundation

The BitGive Foundation, which describes itself as the world's first Bitcoin nonprofit, establishes cooperation with nonprofits like Save The Children and The Water Project.

In March 2016, BitGive unveiled a water well at a girls' school in Western Kenya funded entirely with $11,000 in Bitcoin donations culled from members of the Bitcoin community. "The well serves 500 Kenyans who wouldn't otherwise have access to water," says the manager of BitGive. "It has made a huge impact."[34]

---

34 "Goodbye Corrupt Charity: Hello Blockchain" [EB/OL]. (2016–11–28) [2017–05–18]. http:// www.8btc.com/goodbye-corrupt-charities.

Fig. 4-42: Blockchain plus charities.

BLOCKCHAIN PLUS OTHERS

In fact, Blockchain technology has a wide range of application coverage. It could be combined with any industry that is related to the Internet, including some fields out of people's imaginations.

There are other distinctive fields successfully integrated with Blockchain:

Blockchain Plus Social Networks

Taringa!—the largest content platform in Latin America—launched a revenue-sharing program, Taringa! Creadores. It allowed users to receive a reward in Bitcoin for publishing popular content on their page.

Steemit.com, Blockchain-based social networks, launched a beta version. It uses its own Blockchain and its own cryptocurrency to reward both publishers and curators (those who upvote and discuss the content).

Yours is another distributed social network running on the Bitcoin Blockchain. Its launch was scheduled to take place in late 2016.[35]

---

35 "Most promising Blockchain's application in 2016" [EB/OL]. (2016–08–20) [2017–05–18]. http://www.8btc.com/five-ways-Blockchain-2016.

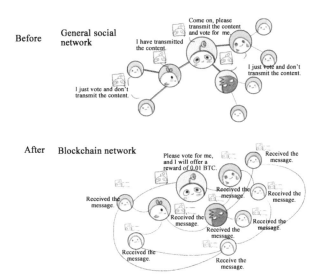

Fig. 4-43: Blockchain plus social media.

Blockchain Plus Games

Takara is a location-based game. It allows users to search for Bitcoins and other tokens—coupons, tickets, loyalty points, company stocks, and anything else of value via a map on the smartphone showing where to look for the artifacts. To pick up the treasure, the user must travel to the exact spot and use GPS. All tokens are registered in the Bitcoin Blockchain and once picked can be used for real-life transactions.[36]

Blockchain Plus Train Tickets

When we buy train tickets via applications on our phones, credit card companies handle payment and charge service fees. However, if railway companies apply Blockchain technology, costs for paying credit card companies will be reduced.

---

36 "Most promising Blockchain's application in 2016" [EB/OL]. (2016–08–20) [2017–05–18]. http://www.8btc.com/five-ways-Blockchain-2016.

Fig. 4-44: Blockchain plus video games.

They could even build the whole ticket service on Blockchain, achieving transparency in ticket purchasing.

Fig. 4-45: Blockchain plus railway tickets.

Blockchain Plus E-mail

If Blockchain can be used to send e-mail, the transfer of e-mail will be more secure. It can even solve the problem of flooding spam because, for spammers, I'm afraid that sending millions of spam to such a security system is not cost-effective. The reason is that in the Blockchain system, the information for exchanging will be verified, encoded, performed, and eventually recorded and stored in a decentralized network that does not belong to anyone. Besides, if the cost of sending mail is extremely low, perhaps people will be willing to pay some service fees for higher security, privacy, and timeliness.

Fig. 4-46: Blockchain plus e-mail.

In conclusion, we can easily see that Blockchain technology could penetrate almost every corner of life. Perhaps twenty years, ten years, even five years or one year later, Blockchain will be integrated into people's lives at lightning speed. Maybe you don't know where you will use Blockchain technology, but it will be everywhere and integrated into your life.

5.

THE EQUIPMENT

Taking on the Equipment:
From Ignorant to Talkative

Blockchain is a comparatively new industry. Honestly speaking, I dare not call myself an elder. Before I decided to do in-depth research on Blockchain, all I knew about it was this was a new term, a buzzword, and a remarkable technology of Fintech.

I started my study by completing two tasks. First, to collect material for a business plan, I searched for all significant events in Blockchain's history, marking them on my calendar. However, on the birthday of Bitcoin, I did not realize the date until midnight. So I jumped out of bed, opened my computer, and made a beautiful poster to celebrate its birthday. At that very moment, all the information I collected on my calendar suddenly became useful. Therefore, the first chapter of the book has been devoted to introducing the historical facts about Blockchain. This book also includes quotations and references from 8btc.com and other Bitcoin online forums.

Second, I studied the terms often mentioned on Baidu and Zhihu. When I first attended a discussion with the OKLink team, everyone was using terms I was unfamiliar with, and I was totally confused. For a beginner, it is crucial to study these terms before participating in discussions. Therefore, in the second chapter of the book, I list the terms I have heard most frequently, and I hope this list will help you to some extent.

A Brief History of Bitcoin: Origin and Future

April 5th, 1975—The birthday of Satoshi Nakamoto.
The website where Satoshi Nakamoto published the Bitcoin White Book is "P2P Foundation." To register on this website, a birthdate is required. It is said that the date that Satoshi wrote was April 4th, 1995. Of course, no one knows whether it was true or not.

1982—The Byzantine Generals Problem.
Leslie Lamport raised the awareness of the Byzantine Generals Problem. The problem is fundamental for P2P communication. The essence is that inconsistency appears when trying to communicate information on an unreliable channel where data are lost. Thus, research on consistency usually assumes

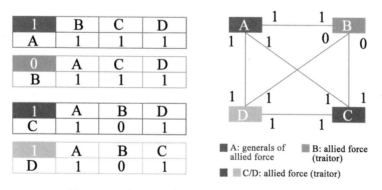

1	B	C	D
A	1	1	1

0	A	C	D
B	1	1	1

1	A	B	D
C	1	0	1

1	A	B	C
D	1	0	1

A: generals of allied force   B: allied force (traitor)

C/D: allied force (traitor)

Fig. 5-1: The simplest consensus algorithm: Byzantine Generals Problem.

the channel is reliable or functions well. Bitcoin Blockchain, born in 2008, solved this historical issue.[37]

1982—The cryptographic online payment system.
David Chaum created the cryptographic online payment system, which focused on private security. The system is untraceable and was viewed as the prototype of Bitcoin private security.

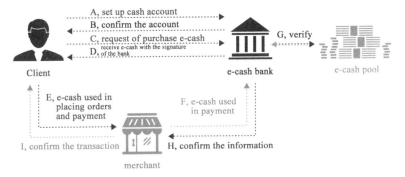

Fig. 5-2: Cryptographic online payment systems.

1990—The Paxos Algorithm was proposed.
Leslie Lamport also created the Paxos Algorithm, which is a consistency algorithm based on information transfer. It solves

	Backups	M/S	MM	2PC	Paxos
Consistency	Weak	Maximum		Strong	
Transaction	None	Complete	Local	Complete	
Delay	Low ratio			High ratio	
Handling capacity	High			Low	Medium
Lost data	Plenty	A few		None	
Fault-tolerance	Down	Read only		Read/Edit	

Fig. 5-3: Comparing Paxos with other algorithms.

37 "The Evolution of Blockchain" [EB/OL]. (2016–04–25) [2017–05–18].http: //tech. hexun.com/2016–04–25/183507891.html.

the problem of how a distributed system reaches consensus or agreement on a particular point.[38]

1991—Timestamp ensures the digital file security.

Stuart Haber and W. Scott Stometta invented an agreement to use timestamp for the digital file security. The concept was later applied to the Bitcoin Blockchain system.

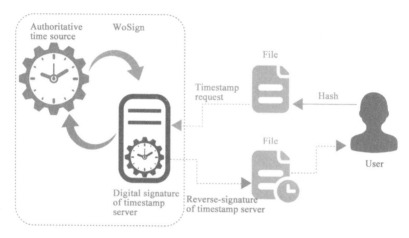

Fig. 5-4: How timestamp works.

1997—Hashcash was invented.

Hashcash, invented by Adam Back, is a PoW algorithm that relies on the irreversible nature of the cost function to be easily verified but hard to crack. It was first used to block spams. Afterward, Hashcash became one of the key techniques used in Blockchain.[39]

---

38 "Distributed Consistency Algorithm Paxos" [EB/OL]. (2016–06–27) [2017–05–18]. http://www.cnblogs.com/cchust/p/5617989.html

39 "BTC Technologies Behind the E-currency" [EB/OL]. (2013–12–20) [2017–05–18]. http://it.dataguru.cn/article-3986-1.html.

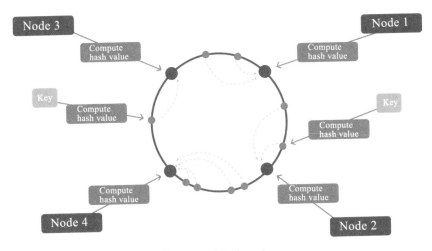

Fig. 5-5: Hashcash.

1998—The distributed e-currency system of b-money.
Wei Dai initiated an anonymous, decentralized e-currency system, b-money, in 1998. The system introduced the PoW mechanism and emphasized peer-to-peer trading and nondestructive features. In the same year, Nick Szabo published Bit Gold, a decentralized digital currency system. Participants could contribute computing power to solving the encryption puzzle. Later, Hal Finney proposed RPoW (Reusable Workload Proof Mechanism), which combined b-money and Adam Back's hashcash, thus creating a cryptocurrency.

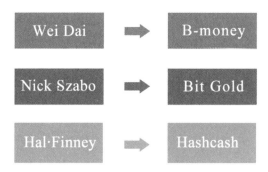

Fig. 5-6: E-currency.

November 11th, 2008—The publication of the Bitcoin white paper.

A Peer-to-Peer Electronic Cash System)一文中提到了比特币。Nakamoto Satoshi first mentioned "Bitcoin in Bitcoin: A Peer-to-Peer Electronic Cash System."

January 4th, 2009—The creation of the Genesis Block.

Beijing time January 4th, 2009, 02:15:05, Nakamoto created the first block in the Bitcoin world—the Genesis Block. In the new Blockchain system, it was set as block 0, while in the old one, it was set as block 1.

Transaction

Time	2009-01-04 02:15:05
Subordinating block	0

Fig. 5-7: The creation of the Genesis Block.

January 11th, 2009—Bitcoin Client 0.1 is released.

On January 11th, 2009, Nakamoto released Bitcoin Client 0.1. This is the first client in Bitcoin history, which means that more people can mine and use Bitcoin.

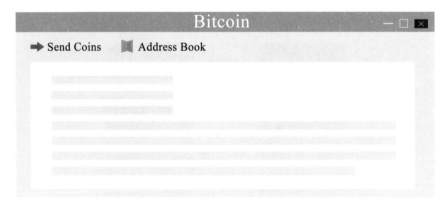

Fig. 5-8: The release of Bitcoin Client 0.1.

January 12th, 2009—The first Bitcoin transaction.
On January 12th, 2009, Nakamoto sent ten Bitcoins to the developer and cryptoactivist Hal Finney. This is the first transaction in Bitcoin history.

Block#170	
Time	2009-01-12 11:30:25
Difficulty	1.000
Total transactions	2
Transfer amount	100 Bitcoins
Reward	50 Bitcoins

Fig. 5-9: The first Bitcoin transaction.

October 5th, 2009—1 USD = 1109.03 Bitcoins
The earliest exchange rate between Bitcoin and the U.S. dollar was 1 U.S. dollar = 309.03 Bitcoins, which was issued by a user named "New Liberty Standard." The value of a Bitcoin is calculated as follows:

The average power required by a computer with a high CPU (central processing unit) operating capacity for one year is 1

1.00 US dollar =	885.91 Bitcoins	10/13/2009
1.00 US dollar =	907.40 Bitcoins	10/12/2009
1.00 US dollar =	867.02 Bitcoins	10/11/2009
1.00 US dollar =	892.52 Bitcoins	10/10/2009
1.00 US dollar =	833.02 Bitcoins	10/09/2009
1.00 US dollar =	922.27 Bitcoins	10/08/2009
1.00 US dollar =	952.02 Bitcoins	10/07/2009
1.00 US dollar =	1130.53 Bitcoins	10/06/2009
1.00 US dollar =	1109.03 Bitcoins	10/05/2009

Fig. 5-10: The exchange rate of Bitcoin.

331.5 kWh, multiplied by the average cost of electricity for US residents of the previous year by 0.113. 6 dollars, divided by twelve months, then divided by the number of Bitcoins produced in the past thirty days, and finally divided by US$1.

December 30th, 2009—The first increase in Bitcoin mining difficulty.

In order to maintain a constant mining rate of one block every ten minutes, the Bitcoin network self-adjusted, and the difficulty of Bitcoin mining increased for the first time.

Block#32255

Time	2009-12-30	13:58:59
Difficulty	1.000	

Block#32256

Time	2009-12-30	14:11:04
Difficulty	1.182	

Fig. 5-11: The first increase in Bitcoin mining difficulty.

July 12th, 2010—The first sharp price fluctuation.

From July 12th to July 16th, 2010, the Bitcoin exchange rate experienced a five-day sharp price fluctuation, rising from US$0.008/Bitcoins to US$0.080/Bitcoins, which was the first sharp fluctuation in the Bitcoin exchange rate.

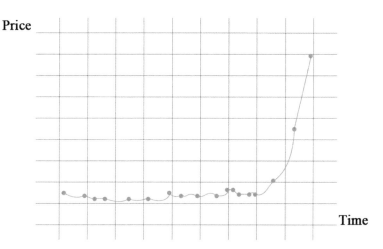

Fig. 5-12: The first sharp price fluctuation.

July 12th, 2010—GPU mining began.

As Bitcoin exchange rates continued to rise, active miners were looking for ways to increase their computing power. Specialized graphics cards have more power than traditional CPUs. It was said that the miner ArtForz was the first person who successfully used an individual OpenCL (Open Computing Language) GPU (Graphics Processor) for Bitcoin mining.[40]

GUI Miner-scrypt alpha	— □ ✕		
GPU threads	1	GPU Defaults	7970 (high usage)
Use stratumc	Yes		
	Stop		

Fig. 5-13: GPU mining.

---

40   "Five-Year History of Bitcoin (Full-Text Update)" (2016–08–13) [2014–01–08].
     http://8btc.com/thread-2603-1-1.html.

August 6th, 2010—The Bitcoin network protocol upgrade.
One of the major flaws in the Bitcoin protocol was discovered
on August 6th, 2010. Transaction information was included
in transaction logs or Blockchains without proper verification.
This loophole was criminally utilized. It generated 184 billion
Bitcoins, and the Bitcoins were sent to two Bitcoin addresses.
The illegal transaction was quickly discovered, and the vul-
nerability was repaired within hours. Illegal transactions were
removed from the transaction logs, and the Bitcoin network
protocol was upgraded to a new version.[41]

October 16th, 2010—The first escrow transaction.
Bitcoin Forum members, Diablo-D3 and Nanotube, con-
ducted the first recorded hosting transaction on October
16th, 2010. The custodian was theymos. On December 5th,
2010, Bitcoin Interacted with the real financial community
for the first time during WikiLeaks' disclosure of the US dip-
lomatic cable. The Bitcoin community called on WikiLeaks
to accept Bitcoin donations to break the financial blockade.
Nakamoto was firmly against it; he thought that Bitcoin
is still in its infancy and could not stand the conflict and
controversy.

December 16th, 2010—Bitcoin mining pool appeared.
Mining became teamwork when a group of miners dug their
first block together on December 16th, 2010, in the Slushpool.
Each miner was paid in proportion to the amount of their

---

41   "Protocol Exploit Generates 184 Billion Bitcoins" [EB/OL]. (2010-08-15)
      [2017-05-18]. http://www.8btc.com/184-billion-Bitcoins.

work. During the next two months, the computing power of the Slushpool increased from 1 400 Mhash/s to 60 Ghash/s.[42]

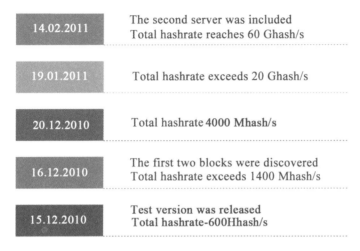

14.02.2011	The second server was included Total hashrate reaches 60 Ghash/s
19.01.2011	Total hashrate exceeds 20 Ghash/s
20.12.2010	Total hashrate 4000 Mhash/s
16.12.2010	The first two blocks were discovered Total hashrate exceeds 1400 Mhash/s
15.12.2010	Test version was released Total hashrate-600Hhash/s

Fig. 5-14: The birth of the Bitcoin mining pool.

June 20th, 2011—A transaction loophole appeared in Mt. Gox.

The world's largest Bitcoin trading website, Mt.Gox (also known as MtGox), displayed a shocking phenomenon in the Bitcoin market at midnight on June 20th, 2011. One Bitcoin was for only one cent, while the normal price previously was about fifteen dollars. Mt.Gox called on the users to change the password quickly and meanwhile declared that all transactions of large volume during this abnormal period were invalid.

June 29th, 2011—The Bitcoin e-wallet.

Bitcoin payment processor BitPay launched its first Bitcoin e-wallet for smartphones on June 29th, 2011. On July 6th,

---

42 "Bitcoin: 'Mining' in the Digital Age" [EB/OL]. (2017-03-03) [2017-05-18]. http://www.fx361.com/page/2017/0303/922619.shtml.

2011, a free Bitcoin e-wallet App appeared in the Android App Store, which was the first Bitcoin-related App for smart-phones and tablets. The App was developed by Brandon Iles.[43]

July 2011—A Bitcoin case unsolved.
In July 2011, Bitomat, the world's third-largest Bitcoin exchange, announced that they had lost access to the file wallet.dat, which meant that they had lost 17,000 Bitcoins preserved for their clients.

November 10th, 2011—Bitcoin POS (sales terminal) was developed successfully.
   POS was connected to the Internet, consisting of a 128×64 pixel monochrome display, a receipt printer, a 24-key keyboard, and a USB (Universal Serial Bus) interface that could connect a QR (Quick Response) barcode scanner.[44]

Fig. 5-15: Bitcoin POS interface.

43   "Bitpay Issued Bitcoin E-wallet" [EB/OL]. (2011–06–29) [2017–05–18]. http: // www.8btc.com/bitpay-launches-e-wallet.
44   "Bitcoin POS Was Successfully Developed" [EB/OL]. (2011–11–10) [2017–05–18]. http://www.8btc.com/Bitcoin-pos.

August 14th, 2012—Finnish Central Bank recognized Bitcoin's legitimacy.

On August 14th, 2012, when a reporter from the Finnish Broadcasting Co. asked about the legal status of Bitcoin, a representative of the Finnish Central Bank replied: "We did not make any promise for the exchange between Bitcoin and the official currency. There is no such guarantee for Bitcoin-like virtual currencies that are out of (government) management."

The reporter then asked: "Is Bitcoin illegal?" The representative replied: "This is not the same thing. People can use any currency they like for investment. After all, Finland is a land of freedom."

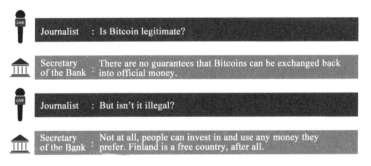

Fig. 5-16: Finnish Central Bank recognized Bitcoin's legitimacy.

September 27th, 2012—The Bitcoin Foundation is established.

In order to achieve the goal of standardizing, protecting, and promoting the development of Bitcoin, The Bitcoin Foundation was established. The foundation is of great significance for media and business-initiated inquiries and complies with relevant laws and regulations.

November 28th, 2012—Block rewards were halved for the first time.

Rewards for Bitcoin mining have been reduced from 50 BTCs to 25 BTCs every 10 minutes. Block #210000 was the first block to be halved.

Block Mtea BTC

Block#210000 parent Blockchain

Time	2012-11-28 23:24:38
Difficulty	3438 361 434
Total transactions	457
Transfer amount	2542170093021 Bitcoins
Reward	25 Bitcoins

Fig. 5-17: Block rewards were halved.

October 25th, 2013—FBI became the new rich in Bitcoin.
The legendary career of Pirate Roberts came to an end. The FBI (The US Federal Bureau of Investigation) took over the 144,000 Bitcoins on his account and transferred them to the FBI-controlled Bitcoin account.[45]

---

45 "FBI Got the Bitcoin From the Silk Road and Became the New Top Rich" [EB /OL]. (2013–10–25) [2017–05–18]. http://www.8btc.com/fbi-ross-ulbricht-2.

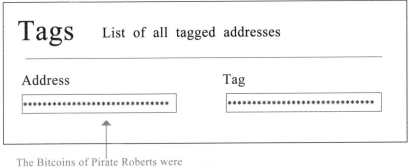

The Bitcoins of Pirate Roberts were
sent to the address under the control of FBI

Fig. 5-18: The FBI became the new rich in Bitcoin.

***November 29th, 2013—Bitcoin price exceeded gold for the
first time.***

On November 29th, 2013, Bitcoin traded at $1,242/BTC on
Mt.Gox, and meanwhile, the gold price was $1,241.98/oz. Bitcoin price exceeded gold for the first time.

Fig. 5-19: Bitcoin price exceeded gold for the first time.

***December 5th, 2013—Five Chinese ministries issued a
notice.***

On December 5th, 2013, five Chinese ministries, including
the Central Bank, issued the "Notice on Preventing Bitcoin

Risks," which clarified that Bitcoin had no legal status as a currency and therefore could not and should not be used as a currency circulated in the market. The day the notice was issued, the average price of Bitcoin plummeted.

December 18th, 2013—Bitcoin price plummeted.
On December 18th, 2013, BTCC and OKCoin, two major Bitcoin exchanges in China, issued a statement announcing the suspension of the RMB recharge service. Subsequently, the unit price of Bitcoin dropped to 2011's RMB price.[46]

Dear users of BTC China:

Because of the well-known reason, BTC China has to cease the function of RMB top-up, but bitcoin top-up, bitcoin withdraw and RMB withdraw functions will not be influenced. BTC China will continue to serve our users. Please keep following our official website and we will soon provide alternative top-up channels. We apologize for inconvenience caused by this adjustment.

BTC China
2013.12.18

Fig. 5-20: Bitcoin price plummeted.

July 9th, 2014—The Polish Ministry of Finance confirmed Bitcoin as a financial instrument.
On July 9th, 2014, Poland's Deputy Minister of Finance, Wojciech Kowalczyk, issued a document confirming that Bitcoin could be used as a financial instrument under the current Polish financial regulations.

---

46 "Bitcoin Withdraws from China? Trading platform Suspends RMB recharge" [EB/OL]. (2013-12-19) [2017-05-18].http://www.kejixun.com/article/201312 /27153.html.

The ministry of finance responded:

> 66 ... and as such, they (bitcoins) can be considered as 99
> financial instruments, according to the bill on financial
> instruments.

Bitcoin's legal status clarified

In the notice, Kowalczyk confirmed that Bitcoin is not an officially
recognized currency in Poland. He said in the policy document:

> 66 An analysis of national regulations allows to conclude that 99
> bitcoin ... is not a legally defined and universally accepted
> currency, because it cannot be classified as either a national
> currency ... or a foreign currency.

Fig. 5-21: The statement from Poland's Ministry of Finance.

July 12th, 2014—France issued new Bitcoin regulations.
On July 12th, 2014, the French Ministry for the Economy and
Finance stated that it would implement regulatory measures
for financial institutions and individual users of Bitcoin and
other digital currencies by the end of the year: "Although the
current scale of virtual currencies could exert an impact on
the economic system, these unofficial currencies are developing and there is a risk of illegitimacy or fraud."

The document read:

> 66 We have proposed [...] a threshold on the margin tax 99
> of €5,000. We believe that France should let people
> try, invest and develop business with bitcoin before
> we tax it.

Fig. 5-22: France issues new Bitcoin regulations

December 11th, 2014—Microsoft accepted Bitcoin
payments.
The global computer giant Microsoft announced on December 11th, 2014, that it accepted Bitcoin as a payment option,

allowing consumers to use Bitcoin to purchase various digital content on their online stores. According to the payment information page of Microsoft's official store, American consumers could use Bitcoin to recharge their Microsoft accounts.[47]

October 22nd, 2015—The European Union exempted Bitcoin from VAT.

The European Court of Justice ruled on October 22nd, 2015, that transactions for Bitcoin and other virtual currencies would be exempt from VAT. This decision was a major victory for the community trading on Bitcoin because it meant that they would not have to pay taxes in the next virtual currency transaction.[48]

December 16th, 2015—Bitcoin securities issued.

On December 16th, 2015, the Securities and Exchange Commission approved Overstock, an online retailer, to issue its shares through Blockchain. According to Overstock's S-3 application submitted to the Securities and Exchange Commission, the company hoped to issue new securities of US$500 million via Blockchain, including common stock, preferred stock, depository receipts, warrants, and bonds.[49]

---

47 "IT Giant Microsoft Listed Bitcoin as a Payment Option" (2014–12–11) [2017–05–18]. http://www.8btc.com/microsoft-adds-Bitcoin-payments-xbox-games -mobile-content.

48 "EU Court Decided That Digital Currency Transactions Would Be Exempt From VAT" [EB/OL]. (2015–10–22)[2017–05–18]. http://www.8btc.com/Bitcoin -is-exempt-from-vat.

49 "SEC approves Overstock plan to issue 50 million dollars stock via Blockchain" [EB/OL].(2015–12–16)[2017–05–18].http://www.btc38.com/btc/altgeneral/8982 .html

April 5th, 2016—OpenBazaar went online.
The developer of the decentralized e-commerce protocol, OpenBazaar, released its first official version of the software on April 5th, 2016. OpenBazaar made P2P digital commerce available and Bitcoin a payment method, which was similar to a decentralized "Taobao."[50]

May 25th, 2016—Japan recognized Bitcoin as property.
The Japanese Senate passed a bill on domestic digital currency exchange regulation on May 25th, 2016, which classified Bitcoin as an asset or property.

June 2016—The General Provisions of Civil Law delimited the protection of virtual assets.
The 21st meeting of the Standing Committee of the Twelfth National People's Congress was held in Beijing in June 2016, where the explanation of the "General Principles of the Civil Law of the People's Republic of China (Draft)," submitted by the Chairman of the Standing Committee of the National People's Congress, was reviewed for the first time. The draft stipulated new types of civil rights for objects like cyber virtual property and data information, where they formally became the object of rights. Bitcoin and other virtual currencies were under the official protection of the law.[51]

---

50 "What is happening in Bitcoin community? From 4th to 10th April" [EB/OL]. (2016–04–10) [2017–05–18].http://mt.sohu.com/20160410/n443807602.shtml.

51 "Virtual asset is officially under the protection of law" [EB/OL]. (2016–06–29) [2017–05–18]. http://www.cnfla.com/gonggao/50131.html.

July 20th, 2016—Bitcoin rewards were halved for the second time.

The 420,000th block was mined, and the block rewards embraced the second halving on July 20th, 2016, and successfully fell to 12.5 Bitcoins. Since the previous halving took place in the second 10,000th block, the currency inflation rate at that time fell to 8.3 percent from 12.5 percent, while the halving of the award occurred in the 420,000th block and the inflation rate fell to 4.17 percent. The subsequent halving of the reward will be in the 630,000th block about four years later.[52]

The 420,000th block has been mined

Fig. 5-23: Bitcoin rewards are halved for the second time.

February 2017—The test run of China Central Bank's digital currency.

The People's Bank of China might become the world's first central bank to issue digital currencies and put them into real-world applications. It was reported that the Blockchain-based digital invoice-trading platform promoted by the Central Bank had been tested successfully. The legal digital currency

---

52 "Bitcoin price fluctuate drastically after second halving" [EB/OL]. (2016-07-10)[2017-05-18].http://www.8btc.com/halving_megathread_block.

issued by the Central Bank has gone through a test run on this platform.[53]

BLOCKCHAIN TERMS: A MUST-HAVE MANUAL FOR EVERYONE

Blockchain

This term is the one that everybody should be familiar with, since many prefer to address Blockchain by its English name. A recent vote changed it to "public credibility chain," yet "Blockchain" remains its most common name. As the underlying technology for Bitcoin, Blockchain is a decentralized distributed ledger system. It is also juxtaposed with artificial intelligence and big data as the three giants of financial technology.

Bitcoin

This term is likely the most one frequently mentioned in the Blockchain field. Bitcoin is the first implemented application based on Blockchain technology. It was originally a virtual currency built on the top of a P2P network, but in many countries, it can already be used to purchase real-life items. Today, Bitcoin has evolved into an open source software designed and developed on the basis of Satoshi Nakamoto's ideas, and a P2P network built on such software.

Satoshi Nakamoto

This is a name one will inevitably encounter while exploring Blockchain. It is the name of the developer and founder of

---

53   "The central bank's digital currency indeed arrived, the industry gives praise but problems are still to be solved" [EB/OL]. (2017–02–09)[2017–05–18]. http://www.cs.com.cn/xwzx/jr/201702/t20170209_5172817.html.

Bitcoin. In 2008, in a mail group that discussed information encryption, Nakamoto published an article outlining the basic framework of the Bitcoin system. In 2009, he established an open source project for the system, officially announcing the birth of Bitcoin. However, after Bitcoin gradually developed into a phenomenon, Nakamoto disappeared from the Internet. Many of Bitcoin's "anniversaries" are related to Satoshi Nakamoto.

Digital Currencies

Digital currency is the initial application form of Blockchain. It is an alternative currency specified in digital form, and both digital gold currencies and cryptocurrencies belong to digital currencies. It is not entirely equivalent to virtual currency in the virtual world, because it is often used for trading real goods and services, not simply confined to virtual spaces such as online games. There are now thousands of digital currencies in the world.

PoW

If you love learning and want to go a bit further to understand the principles of Blockchain, then you will undoubtedly encounter this term, which means "proof of work." Bitcoin employs the PoW mechanism during the generation process of blocks. A qualified hash value of a block consists of numerous leading zeros, the number of which depends on the difficulty of the network. To get a reasonable hash value of a block requires a significant amount of trial and calculation, and the calculation time depends on a machine's hash operation speed.[54]

---

54 "Principles of Bitcoin" [EB/OL]. (2014–01–26) [2017–05–18]. http://blog.csdn.net/ autumn84/article/details/18782533

Public Key and Private Key

When discussing Blockchain related topics, we often see these two terms: public key and private key. These are commonly known as asymmetric cryptography, which is an improvement over the previous symmetric cryptography (using usernames and passwords).

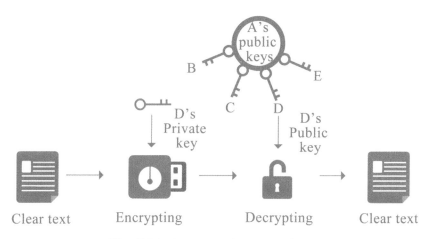

Fig. 5-24: Asymmetric encryption.

In the Bitcoin system, a private key is essentially an array that comprises 32 bytes. Public keys and the generation of addresses all depend on the private keys. With private keys, public keys and addresses can be generated, and Bitcoins at the corresponding addresses can be accessed and used.

Hash Value

Hash value is a ubiquitous term in the Bitcoin world. The hash algorithm maps an arbitrary-length binary value to a fixed-length and smaller binary value, which is called hash value, a unique and extremely compact numerical representation of a piece of data. Even with just a change of one letter in a plain text, the hash values produced subsequently vary to a great extent. To find two different inputs that produce the same hash value is basically impossible from a computational point of view.[55]

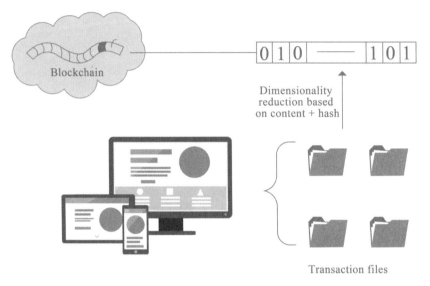

Fig. 5-25: Blockchain dimensionality reduction + hash.

Public and Private Blockchains

People in the industry are often asked, "I heard that you have some understanding of Blockchains, come come, help me out with the classification, is this application a public or private Blockchain?"

A public Blockchain refers to a Blockchain that can be read by anyone in the world, and in which anyone can send transaction information, transactions can be validly confirmed, and anyone can participate in the consensus process. The

---

55 "What Is Hash Value?" [EB/OL]. [2017-05-18].http://product.pconline.com. cn/ itbk/software/dnwt/1504/6325876.html.

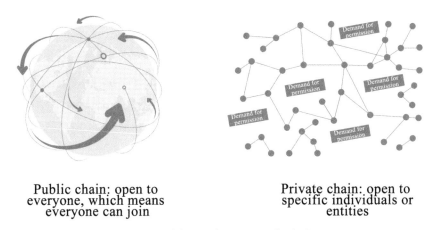

Public chain: open to
everyone, which means
everyone can join   Private chain: open to
                                     specific individuals or
                                     entities

Fig. 5-26: Public and private Blockchains.

consensus process determines which block can be added to
Blockchain, and it also allows participants to understand
the current status. Public Blockchains are usually considered
completely decentralized, while private Blockchains refer to
Blockchains whose writing permission belongs to only one
organization.

In a nutshell, public Blockchains are open to everyone, and
anyone can participate in them, yet private Blockchains are
open to only one individual or entity.[56]

Blocks and Chains

Blocks refer to information blocks. Each block contains three
elements, namely, the ID of the block, several transaction
orders, and the ID of the previous block.

The Bitcoin system creates one block approximately every
ten minutes, and the block contains all the transactions that

56 "A Comprehensive Introduction to Blockchain: Public Blockchain vs Private
    Blockchain" [EB/OL]. (2016–08–09) [2017–05–18]. http://www.weiyangx.com
    /199778.html.

occur across the entire network during this period. Each block also contains the ID of the previous block, which allows each block to find its previous node, and in such a reverse manner, a complete transaction chain is formed. Since its birth to the present day, there is one unique main Blockchain in the entire network.

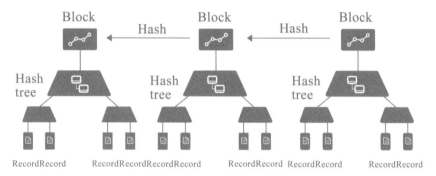

Fig. 5-27: Blocks and chains.

Smart Contracts

The smart contract is also a familiar term, and it seems both easy and difficult to understand. Literally, it means an automatically executed and somewhat clever contract.

Nick Szabo, the inventor of smart contract, defined it as such: "A smart contract is a set of promises, specified in digital form, including protocols within which the parties perform on these promises."[57]

Proof-of-Credit Consensus

This term frequently appears in reports and conferences on Blockchains. The term "proof-of-credit consensus" always

---

57   What Is A Smart Contract? [EB/OL]. (2014–12–14) [2017–05–18].http://www
.8btc. com/ what-are-smart-contracts-in-search-of-a-consensus.

Smart contract replaces implementation contract with algorithms so as to avoid "moral risks" of executive subjects and transactions.

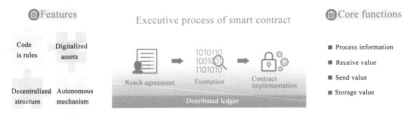

Fig. 5-28: Smart contract.

accompanies questions regarding Blockchain's functions and the reasons why Blockchain could change the world.

The distributed structure of Blockchain and its low-cost trust mechanism based on mathematical algorithms provide a new perspective on solving and optimizing related issues in the financial field. At present, the credit environment in economic society is relatively weak, while the credit cost is relatively high. Blockchain technology proposes a set of low-cost solutions, which are of great significance to the development of the credit economy.

Fig. 5-29: Blockchain's proof-of-credit consensus.

R3

The R3 Blockchain Consortium includes more than seventy of the world's top financial institutions, including China's four traditional financial institutions, namely, Ping An Insurance (Group) Company, China Merchants Bank, China Foreign Exchange Trading System, and Minsheng Bank. The goal is to create a private Blockchain system for financial institutions.

In May 2016, R3 began seeking USD 200 million series A financing for its distributed ledger consortium with its own shareholding percentage being 10 percent. Subsequently, R3 lowered its target financing amount to USD 150 million with its own shareholding percentage increasing to 40 percent, and the remaining 60 percent of the shares were planned to be raised mainly from the consortium's forty-two initial member banks. Then, seven banks withdrew from the financing. Following R3's announcement that it was making its Blockchain platform Corda an open source one, some members, including Goldman Sachs, withdrew from the R3 consortium.[58]

58 "Financing Intensifies Disagreements within R3 Blockchain Consortium: 7 Banks Including Goldman Sachs, Morgan Stanley, and JP Morgan Chase Withdrew" [EB/OL]. (2016–11–29) [2017–05–18].http://www.sohu.com/a/120161115 _115035.

Appendix

What Is It Like to Be A COO in A Blockchain Startup?

—Pan Xiaojun, OKCoin & OKLink COO

In a startup, the COO (Chief Operating Officer) is an engine that never stops. He needs not only to be enthusiastic, but also inspiring for others. Here is what his daily routine looks like:

Talent, talent, talent—finding those with talent is such an important thing; it cannot be stressed enough.

Only those who are reliable can be trusted. Blockchain start-ups without excellent teams are like trees without firm roots, and it takes only a blast of wind to break them down. Like other Internet companies, Blockchain startups also attach great importance to talent and strategies. Strategies lead to products, and products win the market, then the market captures users, and ultimately income and profits are generated. However, compared to other Internet companies, Blockchain startups have more urgent demands and higher requirements for outstanding talents. The people who are needed to explore the rapidly evolving Blockchain technology are those who are perseverant and bold, but also cautious and unafraid to take risks. A good Blockchain company is itself a network of value nodes, and various kinds of professionals who have expertise in product development, testing, marketing, and business operations are all indispensable. The primary task for the COO is to continuously spot talented people and form an excellent team to ensure the company's healthy development.

"What is most important in the 21ˢᵗ century? Talent!"

The same is true for Blockchain startups.

Experienced personnel who can ensure goal achievement.

After all personnel are recruited, like-minded people thus board a large ship that is propelled only by group work. The company's CEO sets a goal, and the COO takes control to achieve it. Weekly management meetings, quarterly performance appraisals and feedback, and annual and irregular shareholders' meetings all ensure that the employees are on the right track and working toward the same goals.

Product, market, and operation join forces.

"What is Blockchain? Can you explain it to me in one sentence?"

"Oh, I see, but what does it have to do with you?"

"How do I know that your digital asset trading platform is reliable? Is your cross border payment service better than that of Western Union?"

"How come my transfer hasn't arrived yet?"

"Gosh! The K-line (Candlestick Charts) pattern broke again!"

"The PBC (the People's Bank of China) issued another document, what do you think?"

......

Replying to various questions from users is also part of COO's daily routine.

In addition, COO should conduct market research: What are the characteristics of the supervision in the Philippines and Malaysia? How come there is a recent huge drop in the click amount and install rate of the mobile application?

In other words, the COO not only interacts with users, but also observes the market, and most important, he works to "attract new users, retain and activate existing users." The COO also needs to work with other departments to manage activities, whether it is to establish online cooperation channels, conduct media promotion, or operate offline business and branding. The COO also maintains relations with the government, cooperates with public relations agencies, and even determine what kind of strategies should be adopted to achieve the goals.

The COO may be the busiest person in a company, for he has to "be able to both develop and carry out strategies," and only those who enjoy taking challenges and solving problems are suitable to be a COO.

DO ALL TECHNOLOGY EXPERTS IN BLOCKCHAIN COMPANIES DREAM OF CHANGING THE WORLD?

—Yu Liang, OKLink product manager and chief engineer

The first time that I heard the word Blockchain was probably in early 2013. As a person engaged in the research and development of Internet technology, I read all the Chinese and English materials available at the time with immense curiosity. Although limited by my English level, I still wanted to understand the principles of Blockchain technology in an authentic way. Today, everyone regards Blockchain as a kind of technology, and at that time I also believed that it must possess some characteristics of technology. So from this perspective, I further studied this so-called "technology." Below, I will talk about my understanding of Blockchain following the three steps of learning, namely, what, why, and how.

First of all, what is Blockchain? Currently, all mainstream media are talking about Blockchain, defining it as a technology. I don't quite agree with this definition; instead, I believe that Blockchain, a new thing, is more like a set of solutions for credit problems. It is common knowledge that currently there are only several credit systems in the world. First is the system based on morality, which is to solve credit problems by way of moral constraints. For example, when we have meals in restaurants, because of information asymmetry, we do not know whether the restaurants use gutter oil or unhealthy ingredients, but we choose to trust the restaurants' owners and believe that they will not do anything harmful to the physical and mental health of their customers. The second system is based on beliefs. I once heard a joke that problems concerning food safety rarely occur in the West, and one of the important reasons is that people engaged in food production are afraid of God's punishment. Since everyone believes in God and that God is a fair judge, a credit system has been established based on such a belief. The third system is based on government. When it comes to government, we have to talk about the banking system of every country in the world. It can be said that they are all based on government. Every citizen believes that his or her government will not collapse and that at any time, a government is a strong backing for its people. As long as the government remains intact, the figures in people's bank accounts have value and can act as a medium for commodity exchange.

After the advent of Blockchain, the cornerstone of a new credit system in the world comes along, and that is the algorithm. The word "algorithm" comes from a computer concept. One of the algorithm's features is consistency, the basic definition of which is that regardless of time and place, as long as the input is definite, through the algorithm, the output must also be definite. Blockchain is a new type of credit system based on this feature of the algorithm.

Second, why do we choose Blockchain? Because it has a number of major features: First, it is safe. From a technical point of view, Blockchain is essentially a distributed database with each data node storing a copy of all the data in this distributed system. That is, each data node independently records every transaction in the Blockchain world. When a transaction occurs, the system broadcasts the transaction to each data node in the Blockchain through the P2P protocol. For example, if there are 100 people in the Blockchain, and one of them transfers money to another person, and the remitter worries that the recipient might lie that no remittance has been received, the remitter then sends an e-mail with the remittance bill and his or her own autograph to the rest of the people. Since ninety-eight people can prove the authenticity of the remittance, the recipient will not be able to falsify.

Second, it is stable. I once heard someone say this before: even the U.S. president, no matter how powerful he is, cannot destroy Blockchain. As the most mature application of

Blockchain, the Bitcoin Blockchain has tens of thousands of data nodes throughout the world. The Bitcoin protocol organizes these nodes into a powerful Blockchain network, so it is very difficult for someone or a particular organization to destroy a Blockchain.

Finally, what do we do with Blockchain? The Bitcoin Blockchain now can make peer-to-peer payments. For example, if you want to wire some money to a friend in the United States, traditionally you need to go to the bank, and the money will be transferred to the United States through the international remittance channel SWIFT, and then it is delivered to your friend through a local U.S. bank. Such a traditional remittance method has drawbacks including high remittance fees, long remittance cycle, and an opaque remittance process. However, Blockchain can truly achieve point-to-point remittance with a short remittance cycle, and open and transparent information, which people can access at any time.

Currently, OKLink is working to build a Blockchain-based global remittance network. In response to the drawbacks of traditional remittance methods, OKLink has designed a global remittance network that features direct payment, low remittance fees, and open information that can be tracked throughout the process at any time. Its remittance services are now available in Canada, South Korea, Japan, the Philippines, India, Vietnam, Indonesia, Singapore, Taiwan (China), Hong Kong (China), and other countries and regions, and they can basically achieve direct payments. It's amazing, isn't it?

I believe that the technological innovation brought about by Blockchain will have an explosive impact on every industry. Let us just wait and see.

IT MIGHT TAKE 100 PICASSOS TO HELP YOU UNDERSTAND THE ABSTRACT NATURE OF BLOCKCHAIN!

—Li Chao, OKCoin & OKLink design director

Born with cryptocurrencies such as Bitcoin, Blockchain is a unique way of storing data. In recent years, there has been an endless stream of innovative applications and designs related to Blockchains. For those who do not work in this professional field, it seems impossible to feel the powerful charm of Blockchain through mere words.

Since 2013, Blockchain technology has been evolving, which greatly interests designers who always love exploring new things. I have always wondered whether visual images incorporating relevant design elements are more intuitive and interesting than boring data and general explanations. For us who are in constant contact with traditional data, this is undoubtedly a new attempt and challenge, and the complexity of the Blockchain technology itself also makes the design work more difficult.

If you want to achieve something, you must first understand it!

A simple design does not indicate a simple design process. It is not easy for designers to visualize Blockchain in a simple and concise manner. In the early stage of design, we put design before data and, by sticking to our original aspiration, developed solutions based on presentation modes. Using relevant packages of Python (an object-oriented interpreted computer programming language), we understood the principles of Blockchain and the concept that transaction history cannot be rewritten. The technology that puts aside banks and uses a verifiable distributed ledger system to verify transactions is simply remarkable. After analyzing and understanding the principles of Blockchain, we decided to use the JavaScript (an interpreted script language) D3.js library, as D3 has a rich variety of icon types and supports SVG format. The data charts built with it are very powerful, and we can use its rich features to fully express the complexity of Blockchain with excellent visual performance. In the later stages, we combined design with data, as visual development should start with simple data. For example, 834 transactions are recorded in block #235235, and such a large number of transactions indicates difficulty in visual performance. So, to ensure that the overall visual design remain unaffected by data changes, we should emphasize data. The purpose of a designer is to make a process clear and concise through simple and straightforward visual design. For example, through a visual system, both the remitter and the recipient can track the flow of transactions during the transaction process.

Visual presentation reduces the difficulty of understanding Blockchain, and we hope that when people see the charts, they can quickly realize that "Wow, so Blockchain is not so difficult a concept to understand." Blockchain is indeed not a new technology, and it only becomes difficult to understand after technical personnel have associated a lot of professional terms with it.

WHAT CRAZY THINGS HAVE WE DONE TO PROMOTE THE THEN-UNKNOWN BLOCKCHAIN?

—Tian Ying, OKCoin & OKLink
brand public relations director

[to match the other parts of this section] Blockchain is a brand-new thing with brand-new underlying technologies, upper applications, and operating principles. Like the Internet, there has never been such a thing in history. Trying to explain Blockchain to the public is just as difficult as explaining the Internet to people in the 1980s.

If you told people in the 1980s that they can shop on the Internet, what would they say?

- Who would want to buy clothes online? It's nonsense.
- I can't even try clothes on while shopping on the Internet. You expect me to pay just over one picture?
- This must be a fraud: those who want to profit from this must be crazy.

If you introduced Google to them, how would they react?

- Free search? Then how do they make money? Must be a scheme!
- This company's market value is $500 billion? Is simple information searching worth so much money?
- More than 50,000 employees are needed for such a simple website? Manual search?

Then what if you tell people now that a programmer writes a program that can change the entire financial market, how will they react?

- It is merely hype for a quick buck, and it will disappear before long.
- Without endorsement from the government, you expect to get notarized simply with a piece of code? You must be crazy.
- There must be hackers behind the operating system. Things that are developed by men can indeed be manipulated!

Don't all these words sound reasonable, logical, and impossible to refute? This is precisely the problem that we are now facing.

In the past year, we went to many cities across the country and organized dozens of offline events and lectures. We went to Nanjing, Shanghai, Shenzhen, and other major cities. We also established booths in places like financial museums, the China National Convention Center, and Peking University. Most of these events were free of charge with the sole purpose of promoting the concept of Blockchain.

After many events, we found that most of the participants were men who fell mostly within the age range of thirty to forty, and most of them were programmers or worked in financial institutions. One unique feature of this group of people was that they were rarely active on social networking sites, and after they understood Blockchain, they tended to use many technical terms when explaining it to others. Using unfamiliar terminology made the promotion of Blockchain progress slowly, and one event could affect about only one thousand people, yet the costs of human, material, and financial resources were very high, not to mention that some of the participants came only for the gifts.

In mid-2016, there were many opportunities in the live broadcast industry with a massive influx of traffic. This caught our attention: promoting Blockchain through live broadcasts must be very effective, and it could encourage many young people to understand Blockchain! We immediately started arranging activities. At first, we asked our chief researcher at Blockchain to do live broadcasts to explain Blockchain. However, after promoting the broadcasts through a variety of online channels, the average number of viewers per broadcast was only several hundred. We wondered why other people's live broadcasts had millions of viewers, yet we only had a few hundred, and no one cared enough to send us virtual gifts. Then, one of my colleagues explained, "You see, the hosts of other live broadcasts are all beautiful, and their voices are all very sweet, of course they attract a lot of viewers!" It made sense. So we invited the most beautiful colleagues in our company to explain Blockchain live. At the same time, we increased our efforts to promote our live broadcasts through online channels and encouraged people to share the information on their social network platforms. Though in the end the viewers reached only several thousand, we were glad to see that we received more virtual gifts and attention from more young people. However, they still did not understand Blockchain, and all they cared about was whether our pretty colleagues had had meals yet or whether they were seeing someone. Promoting the concept of Blockchain still seems like a very challenging task.

Perseverance is the key, and we are still vigorously trying to promote Blockchain through various channels, such as we media, video, audio, books, etc. We hope that Blockchain, the potential underlying technology for financial infrastructure, can be understood by the public and facilitate people's lives just like the Internet.

At present, most of the people who understand Blockchain are employees of large financial institutions or geek masters, which explains why there is a large number of technical terms in Blockchain introduction materials. At the same time, Blockchain itself is also obscure and difficult to understand, so it takes months for a person with no technical background to understand the concept of Blockchain, its history, basic technologies, operating principles, and upper applications.

The purpose of this book is thus to compress the months to a week or even several days.

ACKNOWLEDGMENTS

The development of this book has received help from many enthusiastic friends. We have not only received support from the digital currency and Blockchain industries, but also obtained assistance from experienced professionals and leaders active in the Internet and financial fields.

It takes a long time for an emerging technology to be widely recognized and then applied in society. It is like an individual who wants to be part of a group needing to prove his or her value. Such value needs not to be independent of the system, but to be important for positively promoting collective interests and ecology. Blockchain technology must also prove to possess such value.

Publicizing Blockchain knowledge is the first difficulty that we are facing. The sentence "Blockchain technology is a decentralized distributed ledger" alone will make many readers shut the book. While in face-to-face conversations, when you say this sentence, you can clearly see that the other person's eyes start drifting, and those who can listen to you for more than twenty minutes must be very good friends of yours and are worth cherishing. However, this technology is not as obscure and difficult to understand as everyone believes.

You do not need to understand its code structure; instead, you just need to know what changes this technology will bring about in our lives. This is the original intention of our efforts to publicize Blockchain technology. When changes come, burying your head in the sand does not solve any problems. It is gratifying that we have many companions on the tough road of publicizing and promoting Blockchain. First of all, we would like to thank the president of the Chinese Museum of Finance, Mr. Wang Wei, for his generous help.

Mr. Wang founded the Chinese Museum of Finance and has been contributing his rich experience in life and passion for the financial industry to financial enlightenment and promoting the museum's participation in the future by understanding current developments. The Chinese Museum of Finance has successfully organized many offline salon activities related to Blockchain technology. Mr. Wang gave his warm support to this book at the very beginning and took time out of his busy schedule to write a preface for it. We are deeply grateful to him and at the same time aware that there are daunting challenges ahead.

Integration is the second difficulty. The driving force and mission of Blockchain technology development is to solve the pain points in the traditional field and improve the efficiency of the workforce and capital operation by making use of this emerging technology, whereas shocking headlines containing words like "subvert" and "traditional industries are dead" are mostly to grab attention. Similar to the Internet, Blockchain is an underlying technology, and discussing such a technology in disregard of its application is merely an act of frivolity. The development of Internet technology has significantly improved people's experiences with clothing, food, housing, and transportation, and Blockchain technology will also optimize these experiences.

For example, because of the traceability and irreversibility of data, people will have a brand new experience of tracing the origin of food and detecting art falsification. Besides, by making use of smart contracts and data storage, people will make great progress in the cross platform application of medical data and data privacy. These changes are not inconsistent with the original intention of traditional industries. If social order is an application, then Blockchain technology is equivalent to an upgrade patch, and you only need to click the "Agree" button to enjoy an upgraded experience. Under the influence of the mechanism where public opinion and information are opaque, many traditional industries are slightly resistant to emerging technologies.

However, we consider ourselves fortunate. In the process of promoting technological development, we see the increasingly open attitudes of traditional Chinese industries, as financial institutions, research institutes, and major well-known universities have continuously been sending us invitations for exchanges and communication, which are mutually reinforcing. CITIC Press Group, our old friend, has always been sticking to its original intention of changing the world with knowledge and sparing no effort to help us promote Blockchain technology, for which we would like to hereby extend our sincere thanks. In addition, Mr. Guo Zhenzhou, CEO of Quark Finance; Mr. Guo Yuhang, CEO of Dianrong.com; and Mr. Yang Bing, senior vice president of Mogujie.com all prefaced this book at our invitation and provided much support during the writing process, and we would like to hereby express our sincere gratitude to them.

The world is constantly changing. Some people fear changes, and some accept it. Keeping an open mind and allowing space for new ideas will most certainly make your life more interesting. The changes brought about by emerging technologies are like storms hitting your comfort zone, and if you want to play ignorant to all the sounds, then you can be relieved by closing this book.